Mime the Gap

TECHNIQUES IN MIME AND MOVEMENT

Mime the Gap

TECHNIQUES IN MIME AND MOVEMENT

Richard Knight

THE CROWOOD PRESS

DEDICATION

To Stuart Luis. A fabulous mime artist, who was a great performer, from whom I learnt so much, and who was a good friend.

ACKNOWLEDGEMENTS

Photos taken by Richard Knight and Ellie Cummings
Mime performers in photos: Richard Knight and Ellie Cummings
Book edited by Ellie Cummings
History chapter written by Ellie Cummings

First published in 2018 by
The Crowood Press Ltd
Ramsbury, Marlborough
Wiltshire SN8 2HR

www.crowood.com

© Richard Knight 2018

British Library Cataloguing-in-Publication Data
A catalogue record for this book is available from the British Library.

ISBN 978 1 78500 463 6

Typeset and designed by D & N Publishing, Baydon, Wiltshire

Printed and bound in India by Parksons Graphics

CONTENTS

PREFACE

The Universe had no words in its evolution. It was created with movement. Atoms collided and merged to form existence as we know it. They did not speak to each other first to see if the other atom minded a bit of a bump before they created something new! Mime is movement. And movement is the story of mime. In stillness there is movement. Everything moves. Stillness does not mean doing nothing, stillness is active and alive, a vibration that resonates. Stories are born from movement. A story is the beginning, the middle and the end. The journey from one movement to another, to another.

This book is the result of my journey discovering and learning mime, and the years I have had teaching it in all different classrooms with all different people. I've had the privilege to perform and teach mime for stage and screen, and continue to learn things about acting, movement and presence from my students and my experiences.

I have taught and performed mime for thirty-five years. Along the way I have worked on prime-time television shows, from Bollywood to Hollywood, drama schools, Cambridge and Oxford universities, the National Theatre, the Royal College of Music, the Royal College of Art and the Royal Shakespeare Company. I have performed and taught in the poorest housing estates, with the physically and mentally handicapped, the Deaf Society, with partially blind people and amateur drama societies. I have worked with five- to eighty-five-year-olds, magicians, opera singers, speech therapists, doctors, CEOs, accountants and scientists. People have come to a mime class because they wanted to improve their personal confidence or their presentation skills, or perhaps their partner 'bought' the class as a different kind

of birthday present, or drama students wanted to discover a new skill.

Some people, both professional artists and laymen, turn their noses up at mime: 'Mime artists are scary!', 'I hate mime!', 'Mime is not beautiful,' 'Mime is not real theatre' they say. Some people think that the mime popularized by Marcel Marceau is redundant, that it is a limited art form. Perhaps it is outdated, having been overtaken by performance that is 'socially and politically engaging'. Some people think that a mime show cannot be these things.

Other people can be intrigued by us silent artists: 'Isn't it hard not to speak for so long?', 'Haha! Look, I'm having a conversation with a mime artist!', 'Can you show me trapped in the glass box?' they say.

Everyone is a born mime artist, and there is no escaping it. Mimicry and mime can be both the same and different things. I am not going to explain here the arguments I have come across to suggest that mime is not mimicry, and vice versa. For the purposes of my point, the copying of posture, gesture and facial expressions is part of our DNA throughout our lives. Families inherit each other's idiosyncrasies: that might be a lopsided smile, a certain way of blowing your nose, or an unconscious tic. The mimicry of the people around us literally shapes who we are. The baby watches, absorbs and mimics movement, shapes and expressions in its environment. This is how we all begin to form our brain, and learn about being human.

Jacques Lecoq, the great physical theatre teacher, wrote a book called *Everything Moves*. For me, it is movement that causes all things to come into being: the Big Bang, the birth of stars, planets, oceans, valleys. A thought requires movement, the voice needs to sit on the motion of the breath, all energy, vibrations and frequency are movement. Mime and movement are one. To communicate on any level always takes movement. Movement is so entrenched in our lives that we take it for granted and hardly notice it. The 'pen is mightier than the sword', but 'actions speak louder than words'.

The word 'actor' really means to be the 'Great Pretender'! Acting isn't about displaying real emotions, it's about playing and sharing the biggest game of them all. I like to say we are 'players' who play in the playhouse, performing: this is our game and the big lie that we play to the audience for them to enjoy. The audience goes to the theatre to see the play, so they too can play along and share in this game with the actors. The audience wants to go on a journey into an imaginary, wonderful world, to dream and be moved by what they see and experience.

This book covers all the things I wanted to know about mime, but could never find in a book. So I had to write one. These questions have taken me on a very long journey throughout my career: so often I thought if I could only find a book that could help me! I did find some mime books. A lot of books about mime focus on technique and history. Mime may be featured in general movements books and is mentioned by Jacques Lecoq, Etienne Decroux and Annette Lust – but I've always wanted to know more. I wanted to find that one book that was simple, easy to read, practical, and would provide the solutions to all the burning questions I wanted answers to. So this is my attempt at writing that book I wanted to read in my career as a mime artist, performer and actor. I hope you find it informative and inspiring.

I was liberated from stammering and being dyslexic by becoming a mime artist. The applications of mime are varied and numerous, and I look forward to the day when mime takes a lead role on the world's stage once again.

INTRODUCTION

Our prehistoric ancestors were constantly moving to survive. They used gesture and posture to communicate, and their physical language often mimicked the world and creatures around them. They used sound first, and grew to form words that described the images they saw around them, their feelings, their needs and their relationships. Movement is a fundamental and universal requirement for healthy and sane humans.

Actors are trained to become neutral in their bodies and expressions so they can be part of an anonymous chorus, or can mould themselves into any other character. For the average person, we often unconsciously carry the habits of our ancestors.

Children are very connected to their bodies. They are always engaging with what is around them, and express themselves physically. Their physical expression is their strongest way of communicating when they are very young, and it slowly tapers off as they learn language and how to 'behave themselves' in a socially acceptable way. In the first year of secondary school it is unlikely that an eleven-year-old will hide behind a teacher to express their shyness of the other children around them. This would be seen as 'childish' behaviour, and by this time in our life we have generally found and been taught ways to handle insecurities. As we 'grow up' we may become closed off and defensive. We get body conscious, and keep our heads down looking at computers or mobile devices.

In the Western world most people are so disconnected from their bodies that they have become physically nondescript and inexpressive. We are very used to taking ourselves out of ourselves. We drink alcohol, we smoke cigarettes, we watch films, we turn to spirituality, we spend our time using social media. Most people actively disassociate themselves from their body, and this affects our health, our wellbeing, our personal responsibility and our acting! If we are blocked with connecting to a part of ourselves, how are we going to demonstrate the sensuality or violence that one of our characters demands that we play? The faster that technology connects us to everyone and everything, the less we need to move or go anywhere. We can do everything online, sitting in the comfort of our own homes. Nevertheless we are sociable animals, and are made to move, and to read the physical signals of the people around us, and we love to share our stories and our time.

This separation from the body does not occur within all cultures: it is predominantly a Western concern, and even then it is not spread equally through the Western world. Some are much more connected to their physicality than others. The Australians, for example, seem to have a natural affinity for exploring movement. Technology has some part to play in this, but our psychology also affects how much we sit inside our own minds and bodies comfortably.

Mime is not mimicry alone. It is about physical expression and the body's motion within space so it can be used for story-telling. People express themselves through their movements all the time, the only reprieve being when they are in deep sleep. The interest in the ability to interpret this unconscious expression is prolific – one only needs to look on library bookshelves at the numerous volumes by 'body language' experts to see that people want to tap into the power of understanding our physical expression. These books discuss ways to use the body to trick others or to read other people's true feelings beneath the words they use. They are technical manuals on the body. Each body and each brain is utterly unique. If someone crosses their arms they can be labelled as being defensive. However, what if they are just cold? Or they have a stomach ache? Or they are mirroring you? Or they don't know what to do with their hands? Maybe they are unconsciously hiding their stomach because they think it is big?

There are some things that help in body language awareness, but it doesn't always account for the fact that people act differently at different times in the day, month, year or even in the moment. It's important to be aware of a person's energy level in that time slot, before making a judgement based on their body language alone.

Mime is its own universal language: physical story-telling. We take words for granted, and place so much importance on communicating with vocabulary that we have become disconnected from our bodies. We have become talking heads, detached and disengaged from our physical selves. Ironically, between 55 and 80 per cent of all communication is actually physical. When we talk to someone we look at them. When we go and hear someone give a speech we look at them. We go to a concert so we can see the musicians play. We go to see a film or a play, not to sit and listen.

Out of the five senses that we are born with, 80 per cent of the information that we absorb is visual. That's a lot of visual information that we are processing on a daily basis. Yet there remains a very heavy word- and text-based culture in many drama schools and in Western culture. Physicality, movement and mime is often a minor course, like a tacked-on after-thought to actor training. You can have the best spoken and most verbally articulate actor on stage, but if they are physically inexpressive, the audience will not warm to them. If there is nothing to see on stage but well-speaking actors, why go and see them in the first place? You might as well stay at home, save some money and listen to a radio play.

Sadly, much of theatre today is exactly that: people on stage with well-spoken voices who

move or stand awkwardly. Imagine an actor on stage trying to convince us that he is the strong, victorious King of Denmark: his words tell us he is strong, but his body is slumped forwards, his head is pointed towards the floor, and he drags his feet when he walks. So we don't really believe him. Very quickly we feel we have been cheated, and we might have quiet thoughts that we want our money back, or that we'd sneak away from the theatre during the interval if we were that kind of person. The best moments seen on stage and in film come from how well the actors carry the story and the character through their actions and physicality.

Voice and text are very important, but combined they only make up 20 per cent of what we understand from watching a show. A story can be understood even if it is in a foreign language, simply by the gestures, postures and facial expressions of the actors. Take away the action and it's unlikely you will understand a story in a foreign language, no matter how good an actor's voice is or how well they articulate! You can take away the voice and text and tell a story, but you can't take away the body and speech.

What is mime in performance? It is story-telling using the body as the sole form of expression. The three things we use with the body to tell stories are posture, gesture and facial expressions. For example, a hungry old man walks slowly down the road: we use posture to show he is old, he rubs his tummy to show he is hungry (gesture), and he is sad because he is going to eat his meal alone (facial expression). It is a simple story, which needs to be told simply. A mime doesn't need an old man's costume, because the character is created using his/her movements. A mime may be wearing plain black clothes, with or without white-face makeup, and this will be enough to convey the character and story of this little tale.

White-face makeup is a mask that can exaggerate a mime's facial expressions. It was originally designed for the big theatres and outdoor performances in the old days of Pierrot. Makeup can help exaggerate the facial expressions over a great distance, but it isn't necessary. An expert mime can play all emotions, stories and characters at any time simply by isolating their posture, gesture, facial expression and techniques.

This book should be a quick access guide to mime for stage and screen, for performance and teaching. It aims to answer the most common questions and myths about mime, such as: what is the origin and history of mime? Is mime the same as movement? Is mime about the white-face, stripy-top, French-looking guy I see on the streets? How can mime be applied to acting in theatre and film, how can it enhance my speaking and my body language, and does it affect personal well-being and confidence?

The exercises in this book are suggestions for starting points to find your own path with mime and movement. Students often copy their teacher's movements before discovering what they can do on their own. Starting from a book and being alone in a room somewhere is an excellent first opportunity if you are new to mime. The greatest teacher is yourself: you don't need to find the correct way, just your own way!

1
THE HISTORY OF MIME

This chapter offers a brief look at the history of mime. For anyone wishing to delve deeper into this comprehensive subject, Annette Lust's book *From the Greek Mimes to Marcel Marceau and Beyond* (The Scarecrow Press, 2000) is a great resource with detailed information.

For the purposes of this chapter, the words 'mime' and 'pantomime' are used interchangeably. Throughout history, the use of the body to express emotion and story through posture, gesture, facial expressions and breath has been called both mime and pantomime, and historic references use both words to describe this. 'Pantomime' is not to be confused with the English performance tradition of bawdy, festive performances.

Mime may at times mean to 'imitate', but this is not the only skill of the mime artist, so like much other history, it can be hard to piece together.

ENTERING DOCUMENTED HISTORY

Mime enters written history between 1700BC and 110BC in Indian Hindu texts called the Vedas. Chinese drama was influenced by the Hindus, and a very old Chinese pantomime is said to be about Wu Wang's conquest of China at least 1,000 years BC. Japan's Noh theatre roots may well date from these early times as well. Across Asia, the performance of mime has been carefully choreographed and honed so that even tiny movements of the eye, the breath and finger positions and actions hold an encoded meaning, which the audience has learnt to understand. This technical and detailed method may be likened to Decroux's work

in the twentieth century, three thousand years after its inception in the East.

Mime then crossed the oceans and walked on to the solid, well preserved recorded platform of Grecian terrain. These writings – opinions, reviews, plays and literature – report that mime was an established and well known art form in ancient Greece.

THE GREAT GREEKS

Greece is said to be the birthplace of modern mime. It charmed the playwrights and philosophers, and became recognized across the country, cropping up in village dances, in soldiers' barracks and on a raised area we know as a stage. The ancient Greeks marry the words 'pan' (meaning 'each', 'all') with 'mimeomai' (meaning 'I mimic').

Masks, scripted works and choreographed dances all mingled with mime in the fertile land of Greece, as they always had done and as they continue to do so. Theatre, dance, movement and mime practitioners still debate which belongs to whom in terms of their respective histories.

THE ROYAL ROMANS

Despite these mild contentions between present-day practitioners, the development of mime continued in Rome, where it became very popular. Mime plays were written, and we see the familiar faces of Harlequin and other *commedia dell'arte* characters in Roman statues and art (although at this time they are not known by the names of the Italian characters such as Harlequin, the Dottore or Pantolone).

Roman emperors were caught in feuds about who was the greatest mime artist. Julius Caesar, the famous Roman politician, travelled with an entourage of mime artists, and citizens wore the colours of the mime artist whose side they favoured, in the same way as today's loyal football fans. For a long time mime was adored and loved by all.

However, as with all meteoric rises, there is often a hard fall. As the Roman Empire fell, so too did the popularity of mime.

THE DARK AGES

Here and there in Europe between the fifth and the fifteenth centuries, mime sometimes peeked its head from dingy street corners – but the Church held the lands and peoples in a firm grip, and gradually mime was forgotten, its light and colour fading from memory.

In Europe between the fifth and the fifteenth centuries, there are very few records of mime artistry, as the power of the Church excommunicated anyone caught watching theatre.

It was largely down to performing nomads, who struggled to put food in their mouths, that we now have a rich theatrical culture. They struggled, and suffered for their art, being that it was the only profession they knew, wandering from village to village, across borders and earning what they could, where they could, keeping the traditions of drama and mime alive in scared communities. Our romantic notion of the Bohemian artiste perhaps stems from the Dark Ages.

However, religious dramas (known as mystery, miracle and morality plays) were soon created to educate the populace as to the right and proper way of conducting themselves, their life and their worship, and once more mime had a place on the streets, in village squares and even inside churches. Mime performances incorporated gesture along with song and voice as a tool to engage apathetic audiences in the parables.

Actions and movements are written in Latin in the scripts of such plays, and it was the layman who performed mime actions of the scriptures and dedicated his life to the mime of the Bible stories. Performance began to infiltrate all the Christian festivals, and entertainment sprang up around the country again. Morris dancing and mummers' plays had their origins in this re-emergence of theatre.

THE ITINERANT ITALIANS

Commedia dell'arte is not the subject of this chapter, but its life is undeniably wrapped up in that of mime. The Italian *commedia* actors were such masters of mime that in France, when they performed to the French natives, it is said they were able to understand every part of the story. Indeed it is often remarked that Italian natives were so naturally adept at comedy and gesture that even the village tailor performed a better harlequin than any seen in England, and the troupes were of such genius, they could read the 'scenario' before going on stage, and could perform without need for rehearsal, script or direction.

Comedy, clowning, buffoonery and such were all now ensconced in the performing culture across Europe. Clowns, harlequins and pierrots were seen with 'floured' faces, and this brought mime closer to its recognizable form today.

SHAKESPEARE IS ALIVE!

In the sixteenth century, personified Mime brushes engrained street dust from his breeches, pulls on some new hosiery, and saunters into theatres that have been influenced by the Italian plays. Ben Jonson, Thomas Kyd and Shakespeare all make reference to Mime's exclusive appearance in 'dumb shows'. The Puritan government suppressed theatre, but Mime stepped in as the star again in some dramatic exhibitions by Robert Cox. Performed under the guise of 'rope dancing', these performances delighted audiences all in fear of their own lives for watching theatrical shows. Perhaps it was down to this heroic gesture that John Weaver was motivated to honour a play after him, a pure pantomime, called a production of 'dancing, action and motion'.

GARRICK, DRURY LANE AND LONDON

From the seventeenth century onwards, mime became popular amongst the élite, who rejected 'straight acting' in favour of mime's magnificent ability to demonstrate story and feeling on stage. In R. J. Broadbent's *The History of Pantomime* (Echo Library, 1901), David Garrick wrote:

> They in the drama find no joys,
> But doat on mimicry and toys,
> Thus, when a dance is on my bill,
> Nobility my boxes fill;
> Or send three days before the time
> To crowd a new-made Pantomime.

It is suggested that Garrick's success was down to his outstanding abilities at pantomime. Drury Lane theatre regularly relied on pantomimes for its trade. 'Wiktionary' refers to a pantomime (one who mimics all) as:

> (now rare) A Classical comic actor, especially one who works mainly through gesture and mime.

This brings us nicely to the greatest comedy performer who is still revered today: Joseph Grimaldi.

THE EIGHTEENTH EPOCH

In the eighteenth century Joseph Grimaldi graced the stage with his unsurpassed reputation of being the greatest clown in memory. His mime was imbued with the greatest sense of fun, and as much as he was an actor and clown, he was a mime, and entertained thousands of people.

Friends, colleagues and Joseph Grimaldi's own son continued to perform mime in London through to the late 1800s – whilst across the channel, Jean-Gaspard Deburau was born in 1796. This small young boy struggled to keep up with his acrobatic family. Often falling and stumbling, Deburau left the idea of the circus behind, and found himself outside a stage door. The childlike heart of Pierrot was embodied in Deburau, who carried the years of never fitting in within his soul. Mime helped his inner spiritual poetry be filtered through his limbs and facial expressions, and he found he was able to hold an audience in the palm of his hand. Deburau got his 'break' at the Théâtre des Funambules, which was as much in the dumps as Deburau was when he first arrived there. Jean-Gaspard Deburau carried mime into this down-on-its-luck theatre, and was thoroughly loved by his audience. Of Deburau was written:

> I have never seen an artist who was more serious, more conscientious, more religious in his art. He loved it passionately and spoke of it as a grave thing, whilst always speaking of himself with the extremest modesty. He studied incessantly. He did not trouble to think whether the admirable subtleties of his play of countenance and his originality of composition were appreciated by artists. He worked to satisfy himself, and to realize his fancy. This fancy, which appeared to be so spontaneous, was studied beforehand, with extraordinary care.

THE LAST ONE HUNDRED YEARS

On 6 June 1930, the headline of the British newspaper *The Daily Telegraph* ran as follows (taken from Irene Mawer's *The Art of Mime*, published by Methuen and Co. 1932):

> Last of the Great French Mimes.
> The Great Severin is dead

One of the greatest mimes that France has ever known is dead. The last representative of a school of acting that passes away with him, the Great Severin will play Pierrot no more.

Although the history of mime often only covers Europe, it flourished everywhere at some time or another. America in the 1800s had popular performers and clowns mimicking Hamlet actors and creating mirth for audiences in New York. Russia and Germany (amongst others) had performers who developed their own ways of perfecting the expression of the human body. The great pedagogues Meyerhold and Brecht recognized the importance of using the body to capture the fullness of human expression in acting.

In 1901, R. J. Broadbent in the *History of Pantomime* predicted a surge of interest in mime in Britain. If mime is seen as the silent protagonist of the early silent movies, then he was indeed correct.

George Wague was one such actor in those early silent movies. He had previously played Pierrot on stage, and created his own pantomimes until his debut on screen. He paved the way for mime to move into modern times, and consulted with mime to figure out how best to teach the art and develop performers' bodies so they were capable of creating everything from nothing. Wague and mime made astonishing changes with operatic singers, turning them into excellent actors as well as vocalists.

At about the same time, Jacques Copeau opened an acting school where mime actors started to harness its power. Etienne Decroux took these mime exercises and worked on them extensively, believing that it was possible for the body to express not only what is visible, but all that is invisible, the manifestation of the universal. All that is practically impossible to convey via text, but is experienced and understood by one and all.

Decroux codified movement and named his form 'corporeal mime'. Decroux's students, Jean Louis Barrault and Marcel Marceau, went on to work with mime in different but equally respected ways.

Jacques Lecoq filtered down mime's lineage on the other branch of Jacques Copeau's legacy. He trained with Copeau's son-in-law, and became another great pedagogue. There was always a passive conflict between Decroux and Lecoq as to how mime could be used in the theatre. Whilst Decroux had a language for gesture, Lecoq trusted that a performer could discover for himself his own expression, and that it could be mixed with text, mask, set and lights.

From then until now, students from Lecoq's school disseminated mime's new appearance around the globe.

To this day students and tutors coming from both branches of Copeau's lineage expound their own understandings of mime. Thus for some, the white face is decried, the stripy top expunged, or the street performer scorned. Nevertheless they all have a place in mime's heritage.

MOVIE STAR MIME

Marceau attributed some of his inspiration to Charlie Chaplin, the famous screen actor who incorporated mime with his other talents to produce world-famous films. Jacques Tati is not as known as Chaplin, and is a very popular performer of screen mime, combining poetry and observation with a finesse not often seen in popular culture these days.

In Hollywood, mime became very popular in silent films, and was often accompanied by comedy.

To the movie star mime list we can add Laurel and Hardy, Buster Keaton and Max Lindar. In recent times, Carey Mulligan performed a short mime piece in the film *Suffragette*.

Mime troupes and mime-dedicated festivals have cropped up in recent times, but it is probably fair to say that the masses have not enjoyed mime performances since Marceau entertained them with his character 'Bip' on the television screen.

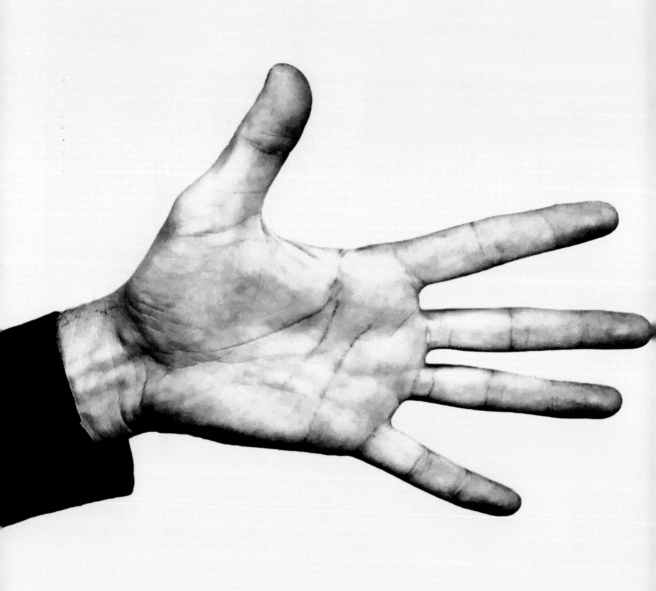

2
BASIC MIME TECHNIQUES

This chapter introduces some basic mime techniques. By doing something simply, you can look really good performing mime. When you first start it can be difficult to control your physicality, without moving too quickly or making actions too busy and unclear.

The basics of mime start to show how our movement creates illusion and meaning. We learn to tense and relax parts of our body at different times, we learn that doing one movement at a time clarifies what we are doing, and discover what stillness can add – and we learn how all these things combined begin to articulate our actions.

GRABBING AN OBJECT

Relax and Tense

The first exercise is holding mime objects. In mime classes you are taught how to pick up an invisible object in a variety of ways, which can seem very 'technical'. This is a way to make this technique easier. I call it 'relax and tense'. Before you grab an object your hand has to be relaxed. This creates contrast to when you do have something in your hand. If your hand is already tense, the audience assumes you are already holding something. The moment you grab an 'object', you need to tense your hand. Tension creates the illusion of weight, shape and substance. When an object is put down, you can relax your hand again. That's it!

1. RELAX: Stand up straight, arms by your sides. Ensure that your whole body, arms and hands are relaxed.

1. Standing in a 'neutral' position.

2. REACH: For a pretend object in front of you, let's say a mug on a table. As your hand moves towards the mug, maintain the relaxation in your hand and wrist.
3. TENSE: Your hand at the moment you grasp the mug. Ideally your hand must open as wide as possible before you grab the mug. (This creates another contrast: opening wide before closing round a shape.)
4. GRAB: The mug by clasping your fingers in a semi-circle shape. Make sure all your fingers are close together. Your fingers and thumb don't complete a circle, rather a semicircle.

5. Toc movement of the mug.

2. Reaching for an object.

lifted from the table. In real life this doesn't happen, but as an illusion, we have to distinguish this moment of separation of the mug leaving the table. This enables our audience to understand the action. The art is to make the 'toc' as tiny a movement as possible: excellent 'tocs' do not draw attention to themselves, and you may not even notice they are there.

LETTING GO OF AN OBJECT

Tense and Relax

This is the same as the exercise above, but in reverse order.

1. With your hand in a semi-circular, tense position, move your arm forwards (or to the side, up or down!) to prepare to place the 'mug' back on the 'table'.
2. STOP: To place the mug on the table, perform a 'toc': pause your movement for a moment. The mug has now made contact with the table.

3. Tense hand.

4. Mug-shape grip.

5. LIFT: The mug up from the table. The important detail here is to create a short, sharp, micro, tiny movement called a 'toc'. This 'toc' gives the impression that the mug has now been

Placing the mug on the table.

Tense hand.

3. RELEASE: Your hand with fingers wide apart and tension maintained. This shows the action of letting go of the object.
4. RELAX: Your hand immediately after 'releasing' the mug. This illustrates that you have let go of the mug and nothing is left in your hand. Tensing your hand and relaxing it should be one natural and flowing movement: one state flows naturally into the next state with no obvious transitions.
5. Bring your arm back to your side.

The basics of grabbing an object and letting it go are very simple. It just takes a lot of practice to make it look smooth, natural and effortless. The technique shouldn't get in the way of the story-telling – it doesn't need to draw attention to itself. The audience only needs to understand the story – good mime can be effective story-telling as well as good technique.

Relaxed hand.

FIXED POINT

I really loved watching the old silent movies of Charlie Chaplin and Buster Keaton. I thought running around and falling over was all you had to do to be funny in a physical way. I had learned how to pick up mime objects, so I thought everyone would now understand my mime performances. The audience did understand when I had an object in my hand and when I let it go, but my stories were still messy and unclear. This was because there was no moment when I stopped! It is important to learn that when motion pauses, it helps to articulate thought and action. This is called a 'fixed point'. When you become still for a second, the mime becomes cleaner and clearer very quickly.

A fixed point is any physical movement that stops momentarily. For example, a policeman puts up his hand up to stop the traffic. A pedestrian stops walking. A professor has a brilliant idea and slams his fist on the table. A fixed point is like punctuation: a full stop that finishes an idea.

Movement comes from the point of stillness, the fixed point. We stop and start again, we start and stop. Fixed points are great for story-telling as they mark the beginning and end of moments in the story.

Fixed Point Exercise

1. Stand up straight, arms by your sides.
2. Turn your head to the right. Look at a spot on the wall a few feet away (this is the fixed point).
3. Continue looking at the spot on the wall, and do not move your head. Now turn the rest of your body to face the same direction and stop for a moment (this is the fixed point).
4. With your entire body facing the same direction (even your eyes!), walk towards the spot until you are one inch away from it. Stop.
5. Repeat the above several times. You can then play around with the exercise – for instance change the height of the spot you look at.

1. Standing straight.

2. Head turns to the right.

5. Changing the height of the spot on the wall.

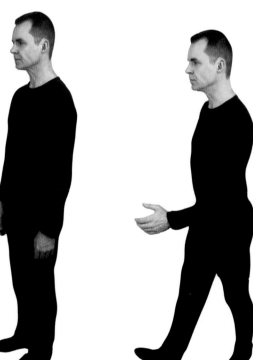

3. Body turns to the right.

4. Walk towards the wall.

6. Change the speed of your movement and how long you stay in a fixed point moment. For example, you might quickly turn your head and see a spot on the wall and stay looking at the spot for five seconds. Then you slowly turn your whole body to face the spot and freeze for three more seconds, then walk quickly towards it.

7. Keep experimenting with different speeds, and how long you stay in any one fixed point.

Any movement that doesn't stop can be called 'continuous'. A continuous movement would be waving goodbye to someone, hovering, or brushing your teeth. If we created a fixed point in any of those movements, it can create humour and disharmony, depending upon how they are played.

Movement that is continuous is like a thought that hasn't yet reached a conclusion. However, all movement does need to come to an end point. (A continuous movement is never unfinished.) Without an ending to the action, the thought doesn't end. In stories, things change, and a fixed point delineates that thought change, new idea or different action. They are vital in mime.

FIXED SPACE

There is another kind of fixed point, which we can call 'fixed space', to save any confusion. This can be used to great effect when performing the mime wall. If used successfully it should look as if there is a wall right in front of the mime artist – their hands fixed to the wall and the rest of their body moving from side to side as if trying to look past the wall.

Fixed space is used to create a mime illusion that usually uses your hands. The hands stay 'fixed' at a point in space, whilst the rest of the body moves around them. This helps when performing a lot of illusions such as the mime wall, and demonstrating drunkenness. Some practitioners call this a fixed point, but for me there is a distinction between stopping or suspending a movement, and keeping a part of your body in the same space for an indeterminate period of time.

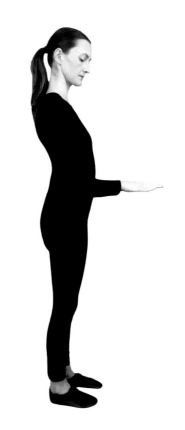

Right arm bent at a 90-degree angle.

Fixed Space Exercise

1. Stand up straight and face a wall, arms by your sides. Imagine you are about to place your right hand on a table in front of you. To do this, lift up your right arm so it is bent at a 90-degree angle. Move towards the real wall so your fingertips are about one inch away from it.
2. Find a spot on the wall that your right hand can line up to as a marker. Keep your right arm and hand exactly where they are, and don't move at all.
3. Now move the rest of your body around your arm whilst keeping it still and lined up with your marker on the wall. Move up and down and then from side to side. See if you can move your body around in a circle both clockwise and anti-clockwise.

Repeat the same exercise again, but now try it with your left arm. Repeat all of the above, but this time try doing it with both arms.

Keeping your hand in line with the mark.

Hands on a mime wall.

4. Repeat the steps above with your hands positioned vertically to the wall plane (with the palms facing outwards) and in front of you, as if you were placing them on a mime wall.

This exercise is a great preparation for the 'mime wall illusion' and creating a mime table.

ISOLATIONS AND BODY UNDULATIONS

Body undulations will be familiar for anyone with experience of breakdancing. Making waves with the body and arms are a part of many dance routines and are the same undulations and isolations that Lecoq and Decroux taught their students.

By breaking down the body's movements and moving them separately, you can see how posture and gesture can create different types of character and suggest different meanings to an audience. Recently there was a documentary about film editing, which showed that the audience interprets the same image differently depending upon what was shown before it. This idea can also be applied to mime: an action performed in isolation to the story gives the audience an opportunity to see a more complex meaning. A simple example might be this: you have picked up a (mime) mug from a (mime) table. You look to the side. You look back at the mug. When you turn your head after those short mime moves, it can make it look as if you have picked up someone else's mug, and you are checking to see if they have seen you do it. Or it could look as if someone has just come into the room. The power of mime is that we can easily add movements in between sequences to activate the audience's imagination.

By breaking down actions, isolating them and defining the body's movement you also become a more effective physical story-teller.

An undulation is a seamless connection of isolations, like the 'waving' movements seen in a lot of dance styles.

As a general rule, you can only do one thing at a time in mime. You look (first thing), lean towards something (second thing), and then walk towards it (third thing). A story becomes a narration from A to Z, and each part of the story is crucial. In each one of those moves, you can add even more detail but stories can be told without that amount of intricacy. At the very least, learning how to isolate the movements of the body helps in cleaning up your actions so that your story is not confusing, messy or busy.

ISOLATIONS EXERCISE: HEAD – CHEST – HIPS – KNEES

1. HEAD: Stand up straight (in neutral) with your arms by your sides and poke your head forwards.

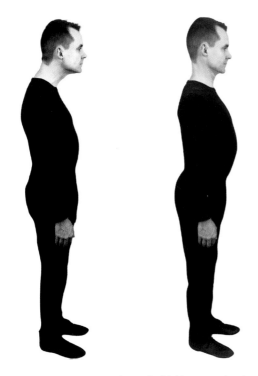

1. Poking your head forwards.   2. Sticking your chest out.

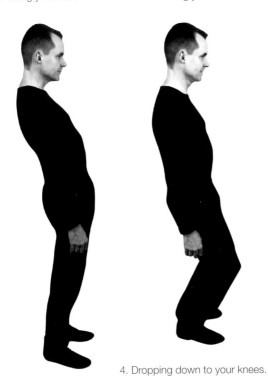

3. Pushing your hips forward.   4. Dropping down to your knees.

5. Rolling up.

2. CHEST: Bring your head back to the neutral position and stick your chest out.
3. HIPS: Draw your chest back to the neutral position and thrust your hips forwards.
4. KNEES: Finally, drop down to sit on an imaginary chair so your hips naturally go backwards and your knees stick out.
5. Come back to a standing position. Simply drop your head forwards on to your chest and slowly stand up as your knees straighten and your body unrolls.

Repeat this exercise several times spending time to really define each part of the body moving forwards and backwards in the space. When you feel comfortable with this exercise, focus on smoothing out the transitions from one part of the body to another.

This is also a great exercise to generally warm up the body. It is easy to stick our necks out, clench our shoulder blades and have tension in the shoulders when moving, so try to be mindful of those 'sticky' points and release them when you notice them. Starting to be mindful about our movement in mime helps us be mindful of our bodies on a more regular basis, and this is very good practice for general health. Congested muscles can create a congested immune system – the blood and lymph systems can't circulate as well through tense muscles as they can through open and strong muscles.

USING BODY ISOLATION FOR CHARACTERIZATION

When training as an actor it can be easy to get stuck trying to create a character, thinking that you have to come up with an elaborate, complex and detailed history. However, sit outside a café and watch real people walking by, and you will find this is a great way to take in titbits of habits and walks, and fuse them all together to form a character. This can be a much easier approach for devising a character. Later on in the process you can learn to create characters by using parts of your body as the leading feature. For example, poking the head forwards and starting to walk can be the starting base for the characterization. It isn't always necessary to over complicate the process by adding particular habits and quirky walks – the head isolation can be more than enough.

It can be interesting to try these exercises and observe how shifting your body position can also change how you feel and what your character's attitude is.

HEAD: Walk around the room with your head as far in front of your chest as you can make it, and let your head 'pull' you around the room. This could be a nosy character, an inquisitive character, or someone who is headstrong.

CHEST: Walk around the room and lead your body with your chest. This character could be a courageous person, a physically strong person, or someone who is forceful.

HIPS: Push your hips out and walk around with your hips leading. This could be someone who is lazy, lecherous or gluttonous.

KNEES: Drop to as close to a sitting position as you can, and walk around the room with your knees leading your body. This could be someone who is old, devious or sneaky.

USING BODY ISOLATION TO SHOW DIFFERENT AGES

Marcel Marceau performed a brilliant routine called the 'Ages of Man', which was simple but so effective. His ability to show all the ages of man so beautifully was captivating. Body isolation can be used to produce a similar effect.

To show the various ages of man, you can use the four basic body isolations of head, chest, hips and knees.

HEAD: To show youth: lead with the head. This could be the physicality of a five-year-old or older child who is very curious about the world. Tilting the head up a bit to the ceiling/sky adds to this impression – it is as if they are looking up in wonder.

CHEST: To show adulthood: lead with the chest. This shows a teenager to a person in early adulthood. They are strong, confident and know what they want in life.

HIPS: To show middle age: lead with the hips. This image can create the age of mid-life when everything 'hangs out' and someone has let themselves go. Physically, the weight of life has pulled them down.

KNEES: To show an elderly person: lead with the knees. This is when the body is too old to fight against the gravity of life and the person on their last legs.

Using mime, it is easy to go through the whole range of the 'four ages of man' using isolations and body undulation. First you walk around the room (or on the spot). Start with the head forwards, looking around in wonder, with the rhythm of a child – free, light and quick. Then stick your chest forwards as you allow your head to go back to neutral and walk with a carefree attitude: this shows the teenager/adult. Then slowly drop your chest back and put your hips forwards: you now automatically walk at a slower pace: this is mid-life. Finally, walk with your knees leading your movement. The hips naturally drop backwards and you walk and move very slowly: this shows the elderly.

To end the scene you can stop walking, sit or lie down on the ground as if you had just died, or start all over again. To explore this sequence further, you can start on the ground and slowly rise to the child position (leading with your head) and begin the entire walk from this starting point.

This scene plays very well with some live or recorded instrumental music, and is a great one for students. Using these four basic body isolations is a very simple and effective technique for graduating from one state to another. It would be best played with clean and precise postures and gestures to accompany the four different physical attitudes. It can weaken the performance if you start adding too many insignificant mime gestures to the piece – for example, talking on the phone, eating some food. The theme of the life cycle is bigger than trivial activity. By keeping it physically simple, it makes for a stronger poetic experience that an audience can imagine and dream about.

USING BODY ISOLATION AND UNDULATION TO MIME DRINKING

I devised a cabaret show a long time ago where I mimed drinking some wine and to show how it travelled down through my body. When I first tried this, it looked a little awkward, as if I was just shaking my body around. I hadn't broken down the journey of the fluid as it travelled down through my body in stages. So I used body isolations to help me. It's an old breakdance move, called the 'body wave', and not only did my movements become more precise, it was funny too.

Exercise to Show Water Travelling through the Body

1. HEAD: Mime that you have a glass of water in your hand. Take a sip from the glass: move your head forwards to take a sip of the water.
2. CHEST: Now stick your chest out at the same time as your head comes back. (The water has now travelled down to the chest area.)

1. Move your head forwards to take a sip of water.

2. Stick your chest out.

3. Push your hips forwards.

4. Drop to your knees.

3. HIPS: Drop your chest back as your hips comes forwards at the same time. (The water has now travelled down to the hip area.)
4. KNEES: Then drop your hips back to neutral at the same time as you go to a sitting position with your knees bent forwards. (The water has now travelled down to the knees area.)

You could reverse the undulation so the water travels back up the body again to your mouth, where you can finish by pretending to spit out the water.

REVERSING THE UNDULATION

From the sitting *knee position* stick your *hips out* as you begin to stand up, then as the hips come back to neutral stick your *chest out*, and finally drop your chest back to neutral. You don't need to stick your head out to complete the undulation, but you can turn your *head* to the side, and mime spitting out the water by making a forward head movement.

USING BODY ISOLATION IN THE SWORD EXERCISE

Whenever telling a story in mime becomes muddling, a good routine to revert to is the sword exercise, devised by Lecoq. It can take a long time to slow down all your movements so that you're not moving too quickly, and the sword exercise helps return to the basics, so that you focus on doing one movement at a time. The sword exercise is about isolating one part of your body at a time, and ending the movement in a fixed point.

The story of the sword exercise is this: you are the defender of a castle and you are trying to find the best sword to use in a fight. You begin with a sword you have just found, and test it with a couple of swings. Then you see another sword on the wall and wonder if this might be a better one? So you grab it off the wall, but realize you can only use one sword at a time. So you drop your original sword and try out the new one. Again you try it out with a couple of swings – but then you see another sword on the wall and reach for that one, and so on and so on.

The Sword Routine

The start position: Begin in the start position, which is as follows: your body is in a sitting down position with your feet placed outside the line of the hips. The left arm points straight down at a 45-degree angle. The fingers are together and hand follows the line of the arm. The right arm mirrors this position, but the hand is miming clutching a sword. Ideally you don't have your fist clenched, and there is space in the palm of your hand. Your back is straight and you look down at your right hand.

1. LOOK LEFT: Look up to your left, at a slight angle. (Imagine a sword is hanging on a castle wall slightly above your head about three feet away, at a 45-degree angle.)

1. Head looks left.

Start. Beginning of the sword exercise.

2. Lunge to your left.

2. LUNGE FORWARDS: Move towards the imaginary sword on the wall by lunging your left leg forwards in its direction. Your left leg is bent and your right leg is straight. As you lunge, relax your left arm and let it drop down by your left side.
3. REACH FOR THE SWORD: Reach for the imaginary sword on the wall with your left hand; your left arm is completely straight.
4. GRAB THE SWORD: Mime the grabbing of the imaginary sword with your left hand. Use the tense/relax exercise from above to add more definition to this action, and avoid making a clenched fist if you can.
5. LOOK BACK: Maintaining this position, turn just your head and look down at your right hand where you are holding the other sword.
6. DROP THE SWORD: You now drop the sword in your right hand by opening the hand up and relaxing it.
7. LOOK LEFT: Keeping the rest of your body where it is, turn your head again and look to the sword in your left hand.

4. Grab the sword.

3. Reach for the sword.

5. Look back.

6. Let go of the sword.

8. FACE THE SWORD: Leaving your left hand in the air (fixed point), pivot on the spot to face your left hand. Swing your right foot around, so it lands parallel to your left foot. You should now be facing the sword square on.

9. SWING YOUR LEFT ARM: Swing your left arm outwards to your left side, then swing it up and across the front of your body, to the right side of your face. The sword should now be close to your face above your right shoulder.

10. SLASH THE SWORD: Slash the sword towards your left side in a diagonal movement. As you do this, bend your knees into a deep sitting position and look at your left hand with the sword in it. At the same time, your right arm shoots out to your right side to match the left arm gesture. This hand is flat and pointing to the ground. Now you are back where you started.

Repeat the sequence once again. Your head will now be looking towards the left-hand side. Every

7. Look back again.

8. Turn and face the sword.

9 (a). Sword moving out to the left side.

10. Your position at the end of Step 10.

9 (b). Preparation for Step 10.

time you complete this sequence of ten moves your body will have moved forward diagonally in space, so after a number of repetitions you will have made a zig zag pattern on the floor.

Additions to the Sword Routine

The time between Steps 4 and 5 is an interesting opportunity as you are holding two swords. You can play around with this moment to tell different stories. What is your reaction to having two swords? How do you make the choice between them? If you were a certain character, how would they respond to this choice? You could look back and forth at each sword as if you are stuck with the dilemma of which sword you should use. You could break up the sequence and try using one sword at a time and swishing it around in the air. What works really well on stage is that you are interested in what you are doing, *not* that you are trying to look interesting. An audience will be engaged if you are, and if you are interested in which sword you will keep, the audience will be interested too.

More Scenarios

Try the sequence and replace the swords for glasses of wine. Which glass of wine tastes better than the other?

Try making up your own exercises, using only ten moves to tell a different story. For example, take an apple from a tree, take a bite from it, but see a better apple and taste the new apple. Try a hat on, but then see another hat/see someone you like, wink at them, then see someone else you like better, and so on.

Try the sword exercise again, or use a scenario you have made up and add some small details. Add a facial expression per move, or a different tempo and rhythm as you move from one step to another.

Repeat the sequence with the detail and play around with your posture and gesture. You can start to build on this story and slowly move away from using the ten moves. By doing this you start to devise a small performance piece. There is no need for method acting or 'actioning' here! (For more information on 'method acting' or 'actioning' there are a plenty of other books available to read on the subject.)

Remember – *keep it simple*!

Great theatre can be created by just using the body. There is no need to get into the psychology of a character and its motivations. Good theatre is how you make the audience feel, and not about how *you* feel emotionally when acting on the stage.

The most interesting part of the sword story is when you have two swords in your hands at the same time. You can play around with this by stopping the routine and holding up both swords to look at each one again, and then testing them out one at a time and making a decision about which one to keep. Once you have decided, you continue with the exercise. An audience likes to watch a character who is interested in what they are doing, rather than when the character is trying to look interesting for their audience.

Do the sword routine again, but instead of using swords, imagine you are in a bar and you see one drink, taste it, like it, but see a better drink – and so on. This exercise can open up a lot of opportunity to create and build even more stories.

USING BODY ISOLATION IN A THREE-POINT BODY ALIGNMENT

Applying mime to acting is simple and effective. I recently had to play over thirty different characters in a one-hour show. In some scenes there was no text, just walking from one side of the stage to the other. At one point I had to walk to centre stage where there was an imaginary border and 'see' a wall that stretched a long way either side of me. I decided to use body alignment to convey the size and length of the wall. I walked up to the wall and stopped. I turned my head slowly to the left. Then I turned my torso, then my legs so that I had slowly turned to face my whole body to the left. All that way over there was the starting point of the wall. To show the full length of it, I turned my head to the right and repeated the process, ending up with my whole body facing to the right. It was a simple trick and highly effective, because the audience 'saw' the length of the boundary without my having to do any unnecessary acting.

Head/Torso/Legs Exercise

This is a very simple head/torso/legs exercise, which can be used for practising body alignment. Begin in a deep squat with your arms diagonally out to your sides.

1. HEAD: Turns 45 degrees to look right – keep your eyes in line with your head as it turns.

2. TORSO: Turns 45 degrees to the right.
3. LUNGE: In the direction of your head and torso – your right knee bends, and your left or back knee straightens.

REPEAT these steps, but this time turn left with your head, torso and lunge.

Try different combinations of moving different parts of the body first. For example, let the legs lunge to the left, followed by the torso and lastly the head. Or go with the torso first, then legs, then head.

The aim of this exercise is to learn to isolate the sections of the body, to make separate movements with each part, and then bring them back in alignment. This is a good discipline to practise, as it cleans up your physical movement so your entire body is saying the same thing when you need it to. If you want to tell the story of your character looking at something, the whole body turns and lines

Start. Beginning stance for the three-point alignment.

1. Head turns to the right.

2. Torso turns to the right.

3. Lunge to your right.

up in the same direction. If you are unaware of what your legs are doing – for instance one knee is bent and your hip is cocked at an angle when you turn towards something – your body posture will convey a meaning to the audience that might not be your intention. It can make your story or character confusing.

Always make sure that your eyes are in line with your head when it turns. The best way to check this is to have someone watch you while you turn your head to the side. If they see that your eyes are not in line with your head when you stop moving, they can gently turn your head to line up with your eyes. This is good partner work. Working with someone else gives you the opportunity to get feedback on your alignment and your own physical behaviours, which you may not be aware of when you work on your own. A partner can also tell if your eyes are moving too fast or too slowly – for instance, your eyes might stop and start at quick intervals as you move around. If you can't find someone to check this, film yourself with a smartphone.

ADVANCED: THE HARLEQUIN EXERCISE

It can sometimes be assumed that to find a strong or grounded presence on stage, all we need do is just imagine we are weighed down, or pretend to be someone with authority. However, this can be especially hard if you carry a lot of 'Air' element in your physicality (see the 'Elements' section in the following chapter). Most artists, myself included, have stomped around on stage in the past trying to find postures and walks that come across as strong and grounded, when most of the time they are half standing up, half squatting, half of nothing, and nowhere near anything, just clumsy and strange looking!

Lecoq's sequence 'The Harlequin' is a set of nine movements, whose postures help to ground a performance: they help you to feel your feet firmly in contact with the ground, and your stance become stronger, helping you to hit the mark every time. This exercise can help an artist become more self-aware and to find new approaches to developing character, as well as becoming stronger in push and pull positions. Your imagination will add to the postures and help to develop new stories.

The 'Start' Position

1. Bend over with a flat back looking straight down at the ground; let your straight arms follow your movement.
2. Turn 45 degrees to your left and move into a backward lunge.
3. From that position, move into a forward lunge position.
4. Pivot your feet around on the spot to the right and lean backwards.

    Now you are half-way through, you are going to do the same moves in reverse order on the other side.
5. Turn to your left side in a mirror image of Step 4.
6. Pivot your feet to the right keeping the body in the same line: this should mean you move into a forward lunge position.

Start position.

2. Backward lunge.

1. Bent over with a flat back.

3. Forward lunge.

4. Pivot and lean backwards.

5. Lean backwards to the right side.

6. Pivot and move into a forward lunge to the other side.

7. Backward lunge on the right side.

7. Move into a backward lunge.
8. Now move back to Position 1, looking straight down at the ground.
9. Finish in the 'start' position.

8. Flat back.

9. Back to the 'start' position.

Repeat this several times until you know all nine moves without hesitating.

Extending the Exercise

Perform the exercise again, but this time add the actions and characters in the following examples. For example, in Position 1, whilst you are looking at the floor with a flat back, mime that you pick up a heavy weight to get you into the next position – and so on.

CLASSIC MIME POSITIONS

Position 1: Lift a heavy weight
Position 2: Pull a rope
Position 3: Push a wall
Position 4: Lean on a bar
Position 5: Leaning on the bar on the other side
Position 6: Push the wall
Position 7: Pull the rope
Position 8: Lift a heavy weight
Position 9: Back to the start position

CLASSIC COMMEDIA CHARACTERS (STOCK CHARACTERS)

Position 1: Be 'pantalone', an old man
Position 2: Play the servant 'harlequin'
Position 3: Play a 'lover'
Position 4: Be the learned professor 'dottore'
Position 5: Be him again on the other side
Position 6: Play a 'lover'
Position 7: Play a servant 'harlequin'
Position 8: Be 'pantalone', an old man
Position 9: Be a melancholy fool 'pierrot'

STORY-TELLING: THE BUTTERFLY

Position 1: Pick up a butterfly
Position 2: Bring the butterfly close to you
Position 3: The butterfly gets away
Position 4: Catch the butterfly
Position 5: Hold on to the butterfly on the other side
Position 6: The butterfly gets away
Position 7: Catch the butterfly

Position 8: Bring the butterfly close to you
Position 9: Drop the butterfly on the floor – it's now squashed!

You can get creative with this exercise if you made it through those examples. Find a love letter, pick a flower, and play the game 'she loves me, she loves me not, she loves me not, she loves me not'.

In each position, take off a petal. Play around and have fun with it. Try doing the classic mime positions of pushing and pulling, but do them in an emotional context. Push someone away or make a gesture to draw them towards you. You can really explore in this exercise because each position is so clean and strong, and your postures and gestures should always hit their mark.

3
THE ELEMENTS

An unusual but interesting question I was once asked by students at the Royal College of Art was: 'What kind of materials are used in mime?' Different materials have different qualities, which leads me to Lecoq's work with the elements. Characters can be portrayed using the qualities of water, air, earth and fire.

The aim of this chapter is to learn the basic qualities of these four elements so you can use them in your mime performances and actions.

WATER

Water is smooth, fluid and flowing.

Exercise to Discover the Water Element

Begin in a neutral position.

1. Lean slowly forwards on to your toes, standing upright; keep your heels on the ground and slowly breathe in.
2. Now slowly lean back on to your heels and slowly breathe out. Make sure your toes don't leave the ground, and that your feet are still firmly flat on the ground.
3. Move around on the spot in a circular motion. As you move around in a circle, it should feel fluid as you transfer your weight from your toes to your heels. Keep your feet flat on the ground.
4. Return to your neutral position and repeat Steps 1 and 2. This time as you lean forwards, continue to lean until you fall off balance – save

Leaning forwards on to the toes.

Leaning backwards on the toes.

yourself just in time and take about three steps forwards.
5. Do the same leaning backwards: fall off balance until you save yourself from going completely over, and take about three steps backwards. Make sure when doing these movements that your feet aren't heavy on the floor, but that they contact the ground softly and firmly.
6. Do the same as above, but this time allow the falling motion to move you around the room in any direction. Allow your arms to swing freely, free of tension.
7. Continue moving around the room. Imagine a different body of water, like waves in the ocean

Tilting to the right.   Tilting to the left.

A heavy water posture.

being whipped up by a storm. Allow your body to be moved forcefully across the room. Imagine a deep, still ocean, and move your body very slightly like the grand weight and depth of a dark, deep sea.

You hardly move at all.

Play around with other types of water: small ripples on a pond create a lighter, quicker motion but still hold a subtlety and fluidity in its movement.

The Water Character

The following exercises are to discover a water-type character.

Begin all the following examples from the 'start' position.

THE DRUNK – THE PERSON WITH TOO MUCH FLUID IN THEM

From standing, lean backwards and forwards, sway ever so slightly in a circular motion (described above), but make the movement very subtle. Let the eyes also roll with this motion as if they, too, are loose and fluid, trying to find focus. Don't play being drunk, allow the element of water to make you move, and let the element surprise you in whatever direction it takes.

THE COOL DUDE – THE PERSON WHO IS SMOOTH AND COOL

This type of character can be played as someone who just goes with the flow, they are an easygoing character. Walk around the room and imagine your arms and legs are half filled with water. As you take a step, feel the weight of the water in your legs. Because the water isn't that heavy you can easily lift them back up again to take the next step. Your arms move with ease with a slight weight to them, but again are light enough to move freely. Play the water element and don't act the character. Let the physicality of playing the water element do the acting for you.

THE DEVIOUS – THE PERSON OR CREATURE WHO MOVES SMOOTHLY TO MANIPULATE SITUATIONS

Walk around the room and bend your knees so you are walking close to the ground. Let your arms make big movements. Imagine you are walking through water that is neck high. Your movements have a fluidity and weight in them. Move your head from side to side and walk smoothly without any quick, sudden movements. This quality of water could be used for fantastical creatures such as those in a fairy tale, or in Shakespeare for a character such as Iago in *Othello*.

AIR

Air is light, free and breezy.

Exercise to Discover the Air Element

Begin this exercise bent over with your arms loose and dangling.

1. Imagine you are a leaf and a slight breeze blows you around very easily. Push off from the toes of your feet and let your arms move wherever they go naturally.
2. The wind blows more strongly and it lifts and moves you lightly and effortlessly around the room (think ballet dancer).

Light movements.

3. Now the wind builds up to gale force and throws you violently around the room in any direction it chooses.
4. Slowly the wind dies down, until you are back into your neutral position with just your arms and body swaying slightly in the gentle breeze.

Beginning position for the air exercise.

You can even get lifted from the ground!

When moving like the element of air, think about the effortlessness of the ballet dancer. They don't land heavily on their feet, and there doesn't seem to be any weight holding them back in their movements. In contrast, water does have weight, which makes its quality become fluid. Air has no weight so it is light, quick and can move instantly in any direction.

The Air Character

The following exercises are to discover air-based characters.

THE AIR HEAD – THE EXCITABLE, FLIGHTY PERSON WHO IS POSITIVE AND LIGHT IN ATTITUDE

Imagine you are in an art gallery. Stand in the room with a feeling of curiosity, looking around in wonder at all the interesting artwork. First, move your head quickly from left to right and up and down at random, using quick fixed points, or 'tocs', a bit like a small bird. See a piece of artwork across the room, and walk quickly and lightly towards it, maybe on your tiptoes. Stop and look around the painting with fast head movements. Turn your head from side to side, poke it forwards and backwards. Then see another fascinating piece of artwork on the other side of the room, and walk towards it with a breath of fresh air.

Repeat this, moving across the room several times. You are so inspired looking at all the wonderful artwork! Carry on moving this way, and then imagine a gale force wind is now blowing you about from one place to another. As with the water exercise, don't 'act' as an excitable, flighty person, but focus on the movement of the air element and allow that to help you find the characterization.

THE PRIMA DONNA – THE PERSON OF HIGH STATUS WHO IS VERY FLAMBOYANT AND EGOTISTICAL

Imagine you are a duke or a duchess who is hosting a royal banquet. You are a self-centred prima donna who is only interested in yourself. Start at one end of the room and move across it with short, quick steps. Your head is held high and your arms held away from your body like a ballet dancer. Stop in the middle of the room, swirl quickly around 360 degrees, letting your arms follow your body with lightness and speed. Acknowledge your guests with a light smile on your face. See someone across the room you want to say 'hello' to, and effortlessly, as if you are floating on air, walk over to them. Keep your head balanced lightly on the top of your spine, and your arms light. Your body is gliding with every step and not bobbing up and down.

Before you get to speak to your guest, see someone else and walk towards them. Get faster and faster as you see each new guest, until you have to pause for breath in the middle of the room. The excitement of it all becomes too much for you (hot air), and ever so dramatically you leave the room on the outgoing breath, with your hands quickly fanning your face to cool down. The quality of this character is all about 'airs and graces'. You are like a light breeze that gets whipped up.

THE ENLIGHTENED MONK – THIS PERSON IS A 'SPIRITUALLY ENLIGHTENED' BEING, CALM AND GENTLE

Imagine you are an enlightened monk who has no cares or worries in the world. You have a light, warm smile and kind, soft eyes. Imagine you are walking calmly down a forest path. As you walk, you head is slightly tilted upwards as you look around at all the wonders in the world. Your arms are by your sides and you are walking very slowly and lightly as if you are walking on clouds. Slowly stop to bend down and pick up a butterfly resting on a flower. As you do this, it flutters away and your head quickly and lightly follows its movement in flight. You can use soft, short, sharp and small head movements to watch it in motion.

The butterfly then lands on another flower. You rise to your feet and effortlessly move towards the butterfly. Before you get to it, it flies away again. Follow the butterfly using quick, light steps to keep pace with it. In a way, you are mirroring the butterfly's ever-changing direction and essence.

The butterfly eventually lands softly on your hands. You lift your hands to your face and look closely at it. For a moment it stays put, and then it suddenly beats its wings and flies off again. You stand, watching it fly away with a light, gentle smile on your face. As it heads off into the distance, your head follows its movement. It becomes smaller and smaller on the horizon and eventually disappears from your sight.

The important thing here is to focus on the light, gentle quality of air. Think fluffy clouds that flit across sky. When watching and chasing the butterfly, if you add the small, sharp movements that a butterfly would make, the audience will be able to see more of the butterfly in their imagination. You can do light, quick, fluttering motions with your hands as your head and body hold no weight or tension in them.

No acting is required. Only your imagination and body is required to create the lightness of a cloud, the quality of the butterfly, and the physical essence of air.

EARTH

Earth is strong, direct and solid.

Exercise to Discover the Earth Element

Begin in a neutral position with a wider stance.

1. Hold one hand open, palm facing to the ceiling in front of you. Make a fist with the other hand.
2. Keeping the open hand where it is, bring your fist up and slap your open hand hard with the back of your fist. You want to hear a sound like clay being slapped on to a potter's wheel. Freeze the action for a moment. Repeat this several times until you make a good, clean, clay-slapping sound. This should make the

Preparing for Step 2.

back of your fist sting a bit, and if it doesn't, then you're not hitting hard enough!

3. Once you've got a good sound happening, bend your knees at the same time. This should all be done as one single movement. Repeat several times, making sure that you bend your knees at the same time as your fist

Smacking your open palm.

makes contact on your palm. As soon as the fist makes contact, stop all movement. Freeze and don't move an inch, not even a millimetre. No bouncing, simply stop everything – as a lump of clay would be when it is thrown on the ground. Be very precise: if there is any movement after impact, this means that your clay has become muddy with the element of water.

4. Move into a forward lunge posture (the front leg is bent and the back leg is straight with both heels flat on the floor). Place your arms and hands in front of you so they are reaching down towards the ground. Imagine that you are picking up the lump of clay that you have just thrown.

5. Turn 180 degrees to the opposite side, lift the lump of clay in your hands above your head, and lift your front leg into the air, balancing on your back leg.

6. Throw the lump of clay, smashing it down to the ground again. Your back leg doesn't move, so your front leg will naturally fall back down to where it was. The key here is that all actions happen at the same time and everything stops at the same time on impact. Keep repeating

Forward lunge, grabbing the clay.

Bending your knees as you smack your palm.

Lifting the clay above your head.

Throwing the clay on to the ground.

this exercise, until you master the movement of throwing the clay on to the floor with your front leg falling and hitting the floor at the same time.

7. Now, instead of rotating 180 degrees each time, take a step when you throw the clay. Continue to step forwards so you begin to walk around the room. Explore this movement to get an idea of the quality of earth walking around the room: it is solid, definite, strong, and making firm contact with the ground.

The Earth Character

The following exercises are to discover an earth-based character.

THE BOUNCER – THE IMMOVABLE PERSON, AS SOLID AS A ROCK

You are a bouncer at a nightclub. Make a wide stance, with your feet rooted to the floor. Cross your arms in front of you, stick your chest out, and tilt your head up. You are solid as a rock and no one gets past you unless you say so. Stand there for a while looking straight ahead like a living statue. After a moment, look to your left and

right, then back to straight ahead. The movements should be sharp, definite and solid.

Now imagine someone is trying to get into the nightclub. As they walk towards you, put your hand up suddenly with your palm facing outwards towards them (like a traffic policeman stopping the traffic). Your fingers are close together: this is a gesture to tell someone to stop where they are. Again, make it solid, strong and definite. Drop your hand down to your side and lift the other hand up in front of you, palm facing upwards: you are demanding to see this person's ID. They give it to you, you take it from them and look at it with concentrated focus for a few moments. Look up at the person and hand their ID back to them. Make each action a fixed point.

Tell the person to go away by pointing in the direction they came from. Cross your arms and imagine they are complaining but walking away. You can just watch them leave. Drop your arms by your sides, then with one arm and finger, point for them to get going and don't try coming back.

That's all you have to do to look like an earth-based character. It is a case of 'less is more'.

A STEREOTYPICAL CAVEMAN

Think of a cartoon caveman. This isn't quite the look we are going for here, but it gives you an idea. Stand up straight, arms by your sides with your mouth slightly open. Walk with feet heavy and firmly contacting the floor. Imagine how a giant walks. You see an object, but you don't understand what it could be. Look at it for a few moments with a sense of curiosity. Keep your facial expression fixed. Slowly walk to the object and pick it up. Try to do one movement at a time. For example, reach for the object (stop). Grab the object (stop). Bring the object up to your face, so you can look at it closely (stop). Look at the object with your head, by tilting your head to the right (stop). Tilt your head from side to side and back to centre, stopping after each movement. Shake the object up and down once or twice (stop). Shrug your shoulders, you don't know what this is (stop). Place it back where you got it from (stop). Turn

180 degrees (stop). See another object (stop). Walk towards it with heavy footsteps (stop). And repeat!

Focus on doing one thing at a time with a slow and heavy pace. The idea here is that in a way you become the lump of clay that you threw in the previous exercise. This is a great comedy character to play, it has physical energy but there is very little going on inside.

With an earth-based character the focus is always moving one part of the body at a time with strong, definite actions. Your job is to make the character believable and real, it cannot be robotic.

THE EARTH MOTHER – A GROUNDED, STRONG AND POWERFUL MOTHER FIGURE

Imagine you are a rural, hard-working Italian mama who has been raised in the country all her life, surrounded by a no-nonsense family. You have to do the laundry (in old-school style), hand-washing it in a steel washing tub. Stand up straight with a solid and slightly wide stance. Pick up the heavy washing tub from a table and put it under your arm. You are going to hand-wash the clothes outside in the garden. As you walk, put your free hand on your hip, and let your hips sway. This adds a touch of femininity to the character. Make sure that your feet make firm contact with the ground each time you take a step.

You get to the garden (stop). Place the tub firmly on the ground (stop). Sit down next to the washing (stop). Grab some clothes in the tub, and then wring the water from them (stop). Repeat this action several times, wringing out the water as if you were breaking a chicken's neck for your dinner, because that is how strong and direct you are!

When you have finished the washing, throw the washing, slap, bang, over your shoulder (stop). Pick up the tub with one arm, your free hand on your hip. Walk back inside the cool house.

The Earth Mother is strong, direct, powerful, and not to be messed with. This character has a great physicality suitable for playing a role such as a headmistress, Lady Macbeth or a high-powered business woman.

FIRE

Fire is explosive, uncontrollable and unpredictable.

Exercise to Discover the Fire Element

Begin in a neutral position.

1. Bend your knees and let your head hang forwards so it pulls the weight of your torso forwards with it.
2. Fire needs air to exist, so take a quick breath in, and pant like a dog that has just been chasing a cat. Fire is unpredictable, so as you pant, make your breathing arrhythmic, let the quick intakes of breath become random and always quick paced and fast. (Do be careful performing this exercise, as it can lead to light-headedness.) Imagine the fire is getting bigger, and increase the number of breaths you take, making them more random as you breathe faster.
3. As you do this, imagine the fire growing inside you, spreading to your arms, then your fingers, your body and your legs.

Starting position for the fire exercise.

Panting like a dog.

Slowly move to a standing position. By the time you are standing fully upright, your arms and body should be flickering explosively in all directions at random.

4. Once you are standing, let the fire (breath) affect your legs in the same way as your arms and body, so your entire body is now moving erratically in random directions. Be careful with your head movements: you don't want to pull a muscle in your neck, just move it in small movements.

The fire is affecting your whole body.

5. Let the fire turn into a complete explosion and a blaze. (Be mindful of your own body limitations and the space around you!)
6. Very slowly, the fire is going to start dying out, so decrease your breath intakes and gradually calm your movements. Come back to your

The fire gets bigger.

The fire is dying down.

neutral position, maintaining a few flickers of the arms, legs and body.

7. Keep the breath intake going as you slow down even more, gradually decreasing them.

8. Finally the fire goes out. Finish with a breath out, and stop to hold the stillness for a moment. Theatrically it allows the fire to go out and die as the air is extinguished.

Another option is to start this exercise by lying down on the floor. Instead of standing up to blaze in a vertical position, you blaze away on the floor horizontally. Fire is random, uncontrollable and potentially highly explosive. This is the one element that some people feel very self-conscious about trying in front of people. You might feel silly and embarrassed. It's normal for this to take someone out of their comfort zone. If this is you, then try it when you are at home alone or in a highly supportive group environment. In the many years I have taught this, there have never been any injuries as we are all quite good at knowing subconsciously not to hurt ourselves.

The Fire Character

The following exercises are to discover a fire-based character.

THE BOXER – THE PERSON WHO CAN MOVE WITH UNPREDICTABLE AND EXPLOSIVE ENERGY

Stand with your knees slightly bent and bring your arms in front of you. Make fists with your hands like a boxer ready to fight. Use the panting breath (as above), and quickly step your feet back and forth as if you are in the boxing ring with your opponent in front of you. Make this fast paced. Randomly strike out at your imaginary opponent with two quick punches, then quickly put your guard up again. Throw out another three fast punches, and bring your fists up in front of your chest again. Imagine the opponent is striking you back, so you have to duck and weave around their punches.

Keep this going for a while, mixing up the punches and the weaving. Surprise yourself and don't think about it. The bell sounds for the end of round one, so you can go to your corner and sit down. Keep the fast breath going. This is the fire of 'fight or flight' blazing inside you, and it's a case of 'kill or be killed'! Repeat for round two. You hear the bell, go back into the ring and start once again. Once you have done this several times (which is a great physical warm-up!) move on to the next character.

THE PARANOID – THE PERSON WHO THINKS EVERYONE AND EVERYTHING IS OUT TO GET THEM

This is similar to the boxer, but this time you use the same energy and level of tension to demonstrate being paranoid of everything and everyone. Stand and look around. Start your panting, but make it naturalistic, somebody who is breathing with fast and shallow breaths. Imagine that someone is out to get you, and you get scared. Take a quick intake of breath, move away from the person and back off slowly to the other side of the room, maintaining your fast and shallow breathing.

Carry on moving away until you hit the wall, an object or another person. This freaks you out, so you instantly jump away, turn around and speed off in another direction. Your breath is going to be very explosive and rapid, your movements will be very sharp and quick. Your movements should be rapid, a machine-gun fire of fixed points. For example: head looks left – right – up – down; body snaps left – right – arms move immediately to protect yourself – feet stumble – quick steps moving in any direction.

THE LOVER – THE PERSON WHO IS PASSIONATELY IN LOVE

Think Romeo and Juliet, and you get the idea of teenage passion at its fiery best. Imagine that you have recently met someone and you have asked them out on a date and they are due to arrive in the next sixty seconds. You are so nervous, this means so much to you and it's impossible to be calm and objective right now.

Start with the quick panting breath, check your clothes, look at yourself in the mirror and sort your hair out. Play with the idea that you can't decide whether to meet them at the door or wait until they come in the room. Initially you feel confident about yourself and you are able to calm yourself down (quick breaths, but they are all in control). You decide to walk towards the door but freak out as you do so, and decide that perhaps that's not the best thing to do after all (explosive quick breaths). Immediately you turn around and walk back to the centre of the room, where you change your mind again and walk back towards the door. Change your mind once more and walk back to the centre of the room.

Play with this scenario for a while, but make sure you don't get caught in a repetitious pattern walking backwards and forwards: fire is arrhythmic. Mix it up, and most importantly, surprise yourself. Let your imagination and your body do the work for you. The lover is fairly neurotic, but positive and hopeful at the same time, so keep it light (air) and explosive (fire).

Fire needs air to exist, so fire is a light element but also highly combustible. If you get caught in predictable rhythms and there is no potential to be explosive, then you will end up with hot air. This doesn't mean you have to explode, but the potential to do so has to be there, and an audience can pick up on this. The best villains have an inner fire brewing inside them, and we know they are dangerous. It's the potential to explode at any time that makes them most interesting.

4
POSTURE AND GESTURE

Buster Keaton was known as 'Stoney Face', because he played his characters with a 'deadpan' expression. 'Deadpan' means keeping a straight face. Throughout his career he observed his audience's reaction to his gags, and found that he got more laughs when he didn't react to the conditions his character found himself in. Charlie Chaplin, on the other hand, and in contrast to Keaton, was meticulous in his pursuit of finding the right facial expression (and gesture) to suit the character that he and his actors were attempting to portray. It is interesting that Keaton could still be a great story-teller without using his face to convey meaning. This has also been used to great effect in productions, with the creative decision to keep facial expressions minimal, and to allow only posture and gesture to tell the story and convey the character's feelings.

A teacher once said 'the verb is the flesh!'. What he meant was that what you say should be the same thing as what you do: your words and your actions need to match each other so your audience is not confused. Deliberately doing the opposite may be a way to suggest subtext, but that can be explored after you have learnt to do the same thing with your voice and your body. Comedy and dishonesty can be played by not matching the text and the physical expression. For example, someone might say 'Yes, I'm fine!' whilst rubbing their (injured) head furiously.

When any person says and does the same thing, we are unconsciously reassured about their sincerity: we engage with them and naturally warm to them.

Posture is like the vowel sound in a word (the feeling), and gestures are like the consonants (the detail). Singers will know that the vowel sound

gives us room to breathe and emote a song. Consonants can take extra breath to produce, and these sounds give the form to the more nebulous vowels.

Posture shapes the body and helps to define age, status, attitude, emotion, even environment at times. Combining the elements with posture can add different qualities such as weight, rhythm and texture. Adding body isolations to posture helps to create sculptured poses.

Let's look at some of the ways that you can use to approach a character's physicality, by developing a posture for them using a single body isolation (head, chest, hips or knees) with a single element (fire, earth, water, air).

POSTURE AND THE AGES OF MAN

This exercise is an intermediate version of the 'Ages of Man' exercise in Chapter 2.

The Infant: Head Isolation and the Air Element

Begin in neutral.

1. With your head tilted slightly upwards, lean forwards on your toes.
2. Open your eyes wide with wonder and curiosity. Add the element of air to your movement (see the 'Air' element section in the previous chapter).
3. Walk around the room with quick steps looking around the room, up and down as if you were

only three years old. See everything around you for the first time.

4. Don't spend too long looking at one thing. Walk quickly towards something, then see something else, and walk quickly towards the new thing.
5. Now find an object, play with it, flick it around, grab it and push it around several times. An infant explores, plays, and tests things out.

The infant has the quality of air, so all movements are quick, light and free. If you spend too much time looking at an object, the level of intelligence appears to increase and the infant will become old very quickly. If you do look in one direction for a longer period of time, this is all right, as older children do this, but the facial expression must be light, open, and free of judgement.

The Teenager: Chest Isolation and the Water Element

Begin in neutral.

1. With your arms by your sides, stick your chest out.
2. Walk around the room with a swagger and a cool, chilled-out attitude. Playing it cool and smooth will add the quality of the water element (see the water element section in the previous chapter).
3. As you walk around the room, see something that interests you and go to pick it up.
4. Look at the object, turn it around a few times, and decide if it has any value to you (or not).
5. If you like the object, that is 'cool', so you keep it. If you don't, discard it lazily and move on to find another object.

The teenager has more physical weight to them: they are heavier than air. Teenagers are more aware of themselves and the world around them, and they know what things are. Make sure you don't look too hard or interested in the objects.

You are looking to find the chilled essence of a teenager that may come across as caring little for things. Teenagers still have some lightness to them, but as they are more thoughtful, there is an added weight. Heaviness and intelligence don't necessarily go hand in hand, though: thus a person with an IQ of 150 wouldn't be played as solid as earth! As another option, you could play a stroppy teenager using the fire element.

The Adult: Hips Isolation and the Earth Element

Begin in neutral.

1. Bend your knees slightly and push your hips forwards with your arms by your sides.
2. Walk around the room with a sense of purpose. Don't rush or drag your feet. Use the rhythm and heaviness of the earth element, with a medium speed pace.
3. See something in the room, stop, turn, then walk towards it.
4. Pick up the object, and take your time inspecting it carefully and thoughtfully.
5. Decide to keep it or to discard it.
6. Repeat the action of finding a new object several times whilst being direct, thoughtful and economical with your movement.

In this exercise you are playing with the idea that as the adult is in middle age, the gravity of life has pulled their body physically and energetically downwards. Movements become slower, more precise and more thoughtful due to the weight of life's experience. An interesting quote states:

> If your energy is low, you are probably thinking about the obligation and not the opportunity.
> *ERIC THOMAS*

Many adults feel obligated, and this affects our energy levels. We become more earthbound. Children, by contrast, have a sense of opportunity and are connected to the potential of change through the elements of air and fire. A standard adult's rhythm is slower and more precise in movement.

The Elderly: Knees Isolation and an Earth Element

The earth element can be used to add weight to this posture. Instead of using a standard earth element on which to base the movement, we are going to use a different type of earth, which will create a different texture. The earth texture for this exercise has been weathered over time so it now has the potential to fracture: it is brittle, which means that it can have snapping movements. Think of the capacity for jagged pieces of rock to break away from worn cliff edges. Your movements are going to be very slow and delicate to avoid that breaking. Bending the knees will sculpt an old person's posture for this exercise.

1. Bend your knees to an almost sitting position. Bend your arms and bring them in closer to your body. Your head is bent forwards towards your chest.
2. Walk around the room very slowly, shuffling forwards as if your feet are too heavy to lift off the floor.
3. Look slowly around the room and see something that interests you.
4. Very slowly, walk and shuffle towards it.
5. Slowly reach for the object and hold it in your hands.
6. Look at the object, slowly turn it around in your hands and decide to keep it or to discard it.
7. If you choose to keep it, very slowly place it in your pocket. If you don't want it, return it slowly to the place you found it.
8. Go on to find several objects around the room whilst maintaining this posture and very slow pace of movement.

POSTURE AND STATUS

Posture is fundamental to playing roles of status. It will be the first thing an audience subconsciously picks up on, whether you are a high-status king or a low-status servant. Some actors have played high-status roles very well vocally, but their physicality has contradicted their vocal quality. High-status characters don't have to move much because everyone moves around them. The richest people of highest status are moved, but their chauffeurs, horses and people move towards them, so they don't need to have a wide range of movement themselves. Playing a high-status character requires you to physically elevate your posture. A low-status character would keep their head down and their body slightly slumped.

High-Status Exercise: The King/Queen

1. Stand up straight, with your chest pushed slightly outwards. Tilt your head up slightly so you are looking forwards over your nose; keep your arms by your sides.
2. Walk around the room slowly, and as you do, push forwards with your back foot from your toes. Pushing forwards with your back foot allows you to keep your height consistently elevated. The idea is that you are gliding around the room, rather than bobbing up and down with every step.
3. Now stop. Slowly turn your head to your left. Keep your head tilted up, and see someone in the room.
4. Slowly turn your body towards them. Gesture for them to come towards you. As you are royalty, make this gesture tiny. You don't have to move much for anyone, it is for them to obey your every command.
5. Watch as they quickly move towards you, follow their movement with only your head, keeping the rest of your body still.

6. Imagine they come to you and bow down. Slowly put your hand out towards them as if you are presenting the ring on your finger for them to kiss.
7. They kiss it, and with a slight flick of your hand, you motion for them to leave.
8. Go back to walking around the room, and repeat this interaction as if you had just entered a great hall with all your loyal subjects waiting for you. Remember to move very slowly all the time with a straight back and head tilted slightly upwards.

This strong, erect posture and slow rhythm can be fun to play with, especially if your character is an evil ruler. It has the potential to add comedy very easily when used with good timing between words and interactions with other characters.

Low-Status Exercise: The Peasant/Servant

1. Stand up straight and slightly bend your knees as if you are going to sit on a chair.
2. Clasp your hands in front of you as if you are holding something in them.
3. Tilt your head down, and sink your chest inwards.
4. Walk around the room with quick, small steps, as if you were looking for food on the streets.
5. See some leftover food scraps in a rubbish bin and quickly scurry over to them.
6. Maintaining the bent-over posture, rummage through the bin searching for something to eat at a very quick and urgent pace.
7. You find something and eat it quickly, as if you haven't eaten for a long time.
8. Now continue to look for more food around the room, on the floor, in bins and in the corners of the room. Always keep the bent-over posture with your arms inwards and close to your body, and make your movements quick.

The low-status character moves quickly, immediately obeying every command to stay out of trouble. They are in 'fight or flight' mode, always looking for food, or career or financial opportunities to better their place in life.

POSTURE AND ATTITUDE

What you think affects how you act physically, and the same is true the other way round. How you act physically will also change the way you think and feel. It's really hard to be confident if your head is looking down at the ground with your shoulders rounded over and your chest pulled in, and you are walking very slowly around the room. In terms of our daily wellbeing our posture is very important for our physical and mental health.

In this section we are going to change our posture to create the visual impression of different attitudes and states of being. As you do the exercises, pay attention to see if they change how you really feel as well.

The Confident Person

1. Stand up straight with the shoulders down, chest slightly out and head up slightly, and walk around the room.
2. Have an inner smile behind your eyes as you walk. Walk as if you are not in a hurry. Nor are you walking slowly either: you have a sense of purpose, and you are walking calmly and firmly around the room. As you walk around the room notice everything that you can see in it.
3. Now find somewhere to sit down on the floor.
4. Stretch your arms out wide and place them behind you as if you were sitting on a beach enjoying the sun.
5. Stretch your legs out in front of you.
6. Now get up and walk around and find another place to sit down and enjoy stretching out your arms and legs as you claim the space for yourself.

The confident person takes up all the space they can physically occupy. Their posture is open, wide and self-assured. This is the person who sits right in the middle of a park bench and spreads their arms wide across the back of it.

The Person Lacking in Confidence

1. Stand up, bend your knees and drop your shoulders down, and pull your chest in.
2. Drop your head down towards your chest, look at the ground and slowly walk around the room.
3. Find a place to sit down on the ground, pull your knees towards your chest and wrap your arms around your legs, placing your head on your knees.
4. Repeat the above several times.

The person who lacks confidence makes their body as small as possible when they come to a place of rest; they don't look at anyone or anything, and they pull their physicality and energy into themselves.

POSTURE AND EMOTION

We can add elemental qualities to our posture, which helps us physically demonstrate emotion. The elements add rhythm and texture to our posture, which in turn creates emotion. There is no 'acting' involved!

Happy: Posture with the Air Element

1. From neutral, stick your chest out, with your shoulders back and head tilted up slightly.
2. Walk around the room and imagine everything that you see is wonderful.
3. See something in the room and walk over to it.
4. Touch it or pick it up and see what a wonderful thing it is. See another, and another, and another

at various points around the room, until you are moving quickly and lightly. Think of the quality of a feather being blown in the wind. We are trying to find a sense of curiosity, joy and wonder.

The 'happy' posture is open and relaxed. Adding the air element will make all your movements and rhythms effortless.

Sad: Posture with the Water Element

1. Beginning in neutral, drop down to an almost sitting position, with your knees bent.
2. Drop your chest inwards and let your arms hang by your sides.
3. Put your head down on to your chest, and walk around the room slowly, maintaining this posture. Think of a slow-moving river, and incorporate its slow, smooth rhythm in your movements.
4. See an object in the room, and imagine that it reminds you of something sad.
5. As you sit down next to it, slowly collapse down into a heap on the floor. Look at the object for a while using very little movement.
6. Slowly get up – don't forget your posture. Walk to another object or point of interest and do the same again.

Let this posture and the rhythm of the water element do most of the work for you. One of the best things about mime is that you can give an audience something and their imagination will do the rest. If you go with the flow of the water element we will see sadness. In a way, mime is like puppetry: it's that magic moment when we see a puppet come to life. Mime does this when the audience starts seeing the things that aren't really there.

GESTURE

Gestures are the details in story-telling, mainly done with the hands and arms. Sometimes a gesture is also made using posture as well, but for now keep it simple and focus on gesture with the hands only. An example of gesture is a police traffic officer standing still in the middle of the road and directing the traffic around them. They use their hands to motion traffic forwards or to stop.

When your body is still and only your hands are moving it can be fascinating to watch. Some of the best moments on stage or in film is when the actor does very little. The saying 'more is less' gives the audience time to absorb more about the character – they have the time to focus on isolated movements. The following are some examples where you can use isolated gestures to convey particular things in a story.

The Nervous Person

1. Imagine you are at work and you are waiting for your boss to come through the door and tell you off.
2. You can either stand or sit for this.
3. Look at the door through which the boss is going to walk into the room.
4. Place your hands in your lap.
5. Staying very still, just move your fingers only, very slightly, one at time. Keep looking at the door.
6. You become more nervous. Quickly start to tap all your fingers on your legs, as if you are playing the keys on a piano very rapidly.

When the rest of the body doesn't move, the audience will be forced to look at the only thing that is moving, which will be your tapping fingers. All the tension and nervousness you feel is now spilling out through your fingers.

Someone Searching

1. Stand up straight and imagine that you have lost your house keys.

2. Drop your head down to your left side and place your hands on your hips in two separate moves.
3. Search for your keys on your body using only your arms and hands.
4. Imagine you have top, side and back pockets in your trousers too.
5. Double check all these pockets, keeping your head looking down to your left.
6. Finally, let your fingers do the searching for you, as if they were little legs for your hands that are walking all over your body, rummaging through all your pockets.

Someone Thinking

1. Imagine you are a scientist and you are trying to solve the riddle of the theory of the universe.
2. Stand up straight, with your head looking up slightly to your right-hand side, and imagine your mind is full of ideas and mathematical equations.
3. Now, let your hands tell the story, by using your fingers to tap away at an imaginary calculator in the air.
4. Make big swiping gestures with your arms and hands, quickly create the solar system in the air, include the sun, Saturn, Jupiter, the moon, the earth and so on. Make sure the rest of your body isn't moving, and your head and eyes are still looking up to the right.
5. Suddenly you come up with the answer! Shoot your right arm up in the air with one finger pointed, as if to say 'Aha! I have it!'

If you wanted to add some comedy, you could mouth words like a mad professor muttering to him-/herself. The idea of this scene is that you are physically mapping out what you are thinking with your hands. You could start it all by scratching your chin with one hand, then beginning the sequence from there. There is a lot of play and fun to have with this character. Start with small gestures, and let them get bigger and over-exaggerated.

The Pushing Gesture

1. Imagine you are a famous actor on stage and you have just received a standing ovation from an audience of two thousand people.
2. You run on stage and take your bow.
3. Slowly stand up again as the tremendous and overwhelming applause reaches your ears.
4. Bring your hands together, palm to palm, as a gesture of thank-you. The audience is standing up and they won't stop clapping.
5. Release your hands, and gesture to the audience to stop clapping by holding out both hands, palms facing towards them. This is the beginning of a pushing action, but we are using it as a gesture.
6. They don't stop clapping, so you clasp your hands together again to say thank-you again, and then you push your hands towards them again to quiet them.
7. They continue! So this time you make one very firm pushing gesture towards them, as if you are going to speak to them if they ever stop clapping!
8. Still they persist, so you drop your hands by your side. You place your right hand on your heart, as a sincere gesture of 'thank-you'.
9. You take another bow, wave goodbye and run off stage.
10. Oh! But they are still clapping, so you run back on stage and start the process all over again.

You can use the same push away/stop gesture if you were surrounded by some gangster characters and they were about to beat you up. Or in a scenario where you have just given a really bad speech and the audience has booed you. This gesture can be played in a number of situations, and as always, it is the simplicity of doing one thing well that makes it effective.

The Pulling Gesture

1. Bend down to an almost sitting position with both your arms out in front of you.
2. You are the witch from Hansel and Gretel, and you see some lost children walking towards your sweet-covered cottage. You smile to yourself, licking your lips.
3. Entice them towards your cottage, beckoning them towards you. To do this, imagine you are pulling a rope towards you. Instead of having your hands circled around a rope, open them wide and pull in one hand and then another rather than both at once. Curl your fingers in towards your palm starting with the little finger and the others following like a wave. This adds some extra detail.
4. The scared children stop in their tracks, so you stop the gesture.
5. Change your tactics and offer one hand stretched out in front of you with an upward facing, open palm.
6. Bring that hand across your body and point towards the cottage, as if you are saying: 'This way please!'
7. The children feel safer and walk past you into the cottage. As you watch them pass you, slowly close your hand into a fist, and put a devious expression on your face.

Lecoq talked about the 'push and pull motors of life', meaning the things that push and pull us as humans. We can either push and pull ourselves, push and pull other people (or other things), or be pushed and pulled by outside forces. This exercise can work on multiple levels.

Basic Gestures to Practise

It is always good practice to spend some time focusing on perfecting gestures so you can enhance your story-telling skills. Here are some more examples to try out. Gestures will add detail to the story.

Imagine you are hitch-hiking, and as you stand by the road, you put your thumb out to hitch for a ride. Move your head to watch the car go by and use one arm with your thumb out for the 'hitching' gesture. Depending upon your character and the urgency you feel, this gesture can have many different qualities. Play around with it.

You see someone you know on a crowded street, so you lift up your arm to wave to them – but they don't wave back, so you slowly drop your arm and think 'is it them or someone else?' Go to wave again – but as you do, you suddenly realize it isn't them, so to save embarrassment you drop your arm down and run your fingers through your hair instead. See if you can demonstrate what you are thinking by using only the movement of your arm.

Experiment with other gestures you see people making, or which you notice yourself making, and find out if you can tell the story or convey thoughts and feelings by using only your hands and arms.

Another gesture is shrugging the shoulders when you don't know something, as is yawning. Sometimes another part of the body needs to add to the gesture to complete it. For example, if you are miming that you are very hungry, you can add posture to your hand movement: pull your stomach in, bend your knees, tilt your head down, then do the action of rubbing your stomach.

Gestures and postures should always work together, but sometimes you can focus on one to tell the story more effectively. Once you have had a lot of practice with posture and gesture it's time to add facial expressions.

FACIAL EXPRESSIONS

Facial expressions are the emotional details. Wearing a mask portrays one fixed expression so the actor has to play different emotions using their body. A mime can do the same, but we can change our facial expression at will. A great mime will know exactly when to change their facial expression and when to stay with the one expression. With facial expressions too many changes, too quickly is confusing and messy. So to begin, imagine that you are wearing a mask, and that you are stuck with playing one expression.

Playing Around with your Facial Expressions

1. Stand in front of a mirror, and look at yourself with a blank and neutral expression.
2. Now looked surprised, and hold that expression as if it were fixed like a mask on your face.
3. Look left and right, up and down, tilt your head to your left then your right, making sure you still keep that one expression.
4. Imagine you have lost your keys and that you are checking all your pockets for them. Keep searching for them everywhere while keeping that one expression firmly fixed in place.
5. After a while, stop moving your whole body, and remain completely still. You begin to remember where you put the keys. You can now change your expression slowly from an expression of surprise to a smile.
6. A smile is now your new mask, so keep that expression fixed and search your pockets again and find your keys.
7. You take your keys out of your pocket and then realize they are the wrong keys. Now quickly change your expression from a smile to a sad one. This is now your new mask.
8. You place your keys back in your pocket and look slowly around the room from left to right, and look back again, as your last hope of finding your keys has vanished.
9. You give up finding your keys, and resign yourself to the fact that it doesn't really matter anyway. You shrug your shoulders, breathe out, and slowly let your expression change back to a smile again.
10. Now try different expressions that you can fix in place and hold for a while. See what you can do with this list: fear, anger, thoughtful, jealous, interested, carefree, envy, lustful, devious, confused,

intelligent, exhausted, clever, shocked, frustrated, defiant, regal, sleepy.

Try the suggested list and see how quickly you can go from one expression to the other. Then see how slowly you can change from one expression to the other. The key here is to be very precise, so that each expression is clearly defined and very readable and recognizable. This will take a lot of hard work to do well, but it will give you the ability to convey a lot of expressions very quickly and effortlessly. There is no one way of creating an expression: you must find your own way of doing it, as everyone is different. Ultimately in mime you don't try to play an emotion, but you can add a facial expression that helps tell the feelings in the story.

Standing in neutral.

BASIC ARM WAVE MOVEMENT

The arm wave is a very popular movement that became prevalent in the 1980s during the breakdance craze. Yet performed badly it can look embarrassing!

In this action you send a movement from one arm to the other, creating the impression of a wave. Your arms will look like rubber if it is done well. It can be used in mime at times. For instance, imagine you just touched a high voltage wire – using this move you will be able to demonstrate the action of being electrocuted as the current travels through your body.

Stand in neutral with your arms by your sides.

1. Arms out with your palms down.

1. Bend your arms at the elbows and turn your arms out with the palms facing down. Now move your arms about an inch away from your body. Make sure that your fingers are close together. We are going to send a wave from left to right.
2. Make a 90-degree angle with your left wrist so your fingers point to the ground.
3. Then move your left hand back to its original position. At the same time, move your bent elbow upwards. I call this the 'Egyptian move'.
4. Straighten your left arm and move your shoulder towards your left ear. This is a harder move to do, and ideally you want to keep your hand in fixed space as much as possible.
5. Now drop your left shoulder to a normal position, and let your left arm return to its starting position. We are going to do the same

2. Left wrist points down.

thing again with the right arm, but in reverse order.

6. As your drop your left shoulder, straighten your right arm and move your right shoulder close to your ear.

7. Move your right arm into the 'Egyptian move', as we did on the left side. Your right hand is still flat and horizontal with the fingers pointing away from your body. Try to keep your left hand in fixed space as you move your elbow.

8. As you bring your right elbow back to its original position, make a 90-degree angle with your wrist so your fingers are pointing to the ground.

9. The final move is to flick the hand back to its starting position.

3. The 'Egyptian' move.

5–6. Moving the shoulder to the ear and straightening your arm.

4. Straighten your left arm.

7. 'Egyptian' move with the right arm.

8. 90-degree angle with the right wrist.

9. Back to start position.

Now repeat the moves going from right to left, then back again, left to right. The most important part of this illusion is the 'Egyptian move'. Practise the sequence of moves until you feel comfortable with them. As you get more comfortable you will find it easier to move from one position to the next, and you will naturally speed up. See how fast you can send the wave from one side of the body to the other. You want to get to the stage where the sequence looks like a smooth, single movement rather than a number of steps. Practise it in slow motion because this will help you to be more accurate and to get some flow going without having to make a fast transition from one step to the next.

Try doing the wave with your arms starting further away from your body, which can help create a small ripple effect. Once you have achieved it, play around and have fun with it – see what else you can do using different tempos or just moving one part of the arm at a time. It's a hard exercise to get really good, but once you do, it's a great trick to have up your sleeve.

The Hand Wave

We can now add detail to the arm wave movement with the hands and fingers. Let's break down the hand movement first.

Stand or sit down with a real table in front of you. Place one hand on the table.

THE BACKWARDS HAND WAVE

1. Sit down at a table and place one hand flat on the surface.

    Make a claw with your fingers as if you were scratching the surface of the table. Make sure your fingertips and your palm stay in contact with the table.

1 (a). Hand flat on the table.

1 (b). Making a claw.

2. Making a pyramid.

3. Flatten your hand.

1. Place one hand down flat on a real table. Keeping the fingertips where they are, make a pyramid shape with your fingers; this will make your palm move forwards.
2. Leaving your fingertips where they are, collapse the pyramid forwards so your hand makes a claw shape.
3. Flatten out your hand by rolling your fingers forwards so your hand is once again flat on the table.

Repeat the steps several times: pyramid, claw, flatten and repeat.

Once you have perfected this on the table, lift your hand off it slightly, so your hand is about one

1. Pyramid shape with the hand.

2. Leaving your fingertips where they are, straighten your fingers so the action pushes your knuckles upwards, forming a 'pyramid shape' with your hand.
3. Again, leaving your fingertips exactly where they are, flatten your hand on the table, so you have pushed the palm of your hand backwards. Place your palm flat on the table. You are now back to the original starting position, and your hand has moved closer to you on the table.

Repeat the three stages of the exercise several times: claw, pyramid, flatten and repeat.

The only time that the fingertips move is when you make the claw. This allows the hand to move backwards. Once you have perfected this on the table, lift your hand from the surface slightly so it is in the air, and practise the exercise from here. Complete each step one at a time, until you can do the sequence as one fluid, smooth movement. Try it from the beginning with the other hand if you haven't already.

THE FORWARDS HAND WAVE

This is the same as the backwards hand wave, just in reverse!

2. Making a claw shape.

3. Flat hand.

inch away from the surface. Practise the moves in the air. Carry on until you can make the sequence one smooth, fluid movement without any stops in between. Don't forget to practise the hand wave with your other hand, too.

Once you have mastered the hand waves, you can add them to the arm wave. The arm wave will begin with your fingers first: making a claw, then pushing into a pyramid shape, then flattening the hand. The wave then moves into your wrist. When the wave gets to the other side of your body, the palm of your hand will already be facing down, so bring up the knuckles into the pyramid shape, then make the claw shape, then roll out your fingers so your hand is back to its original position.

5
THE BREATH

It is always good to add the breath into a mime action wherever possible. Using breath with mime adds another detail that can emphasize a physical action or help to show an emotion. I once saw a show where the male character was just about to ask a girl out on a date, and he was very nervous. He came on stage and watched the girl working away at her desk and he just stood there looking at her. He breathed in and held his breath for a moment, and the audience followed suit. We knew exactly how he was feeling because we had unconsciously empathized with him and copied his intake of breath. It was so simple, yet very compelling to watch and experience.

USING YOUR BREATH ON YOUR ENTRANCE

Late for a Meeting

1. Stand outside a room and imagine you are late for a meeting.
2. Breathe in first before walking into the room.
3. Hold your breath for a moment, ready for the worst.
4. Pretend that your boss is really happy with you and wants to give you a pay rise. So you breathe out, relieved.

The Wrong Room

1. You are about to see a good friend in the office. Breathe out before you go into the room.

2. But you've gone into the wrong room and have just walked into a major board meeting. Breathe in and exit quickly, holding your breath.

You can find a lot of comedy in a scene by using your breath. If you breathe in, the audience will have a sense of breathing in as well. When you breathe out, they may also have the same feeling of exhalation. What you give the audience, they receive. It's a very simple principle to bear in mind with all your performances.

An Exit

1. Stand in the middle of the room and imagine that someone has just insulted you.
2. Breathe in and walk out of the room disgusted.

Another Exit

1. Imagine that you have left the gas on at home. You start to get worried and breathe in.
2. Then you realize it's all right because you remember that you turned the gas off before you left the house, so you breathe out and continue as you were.

Other Ideas

Someone you fancy has come into the room and you breathe in. As they leave, you sigh the air out.

Imagine you come into the room and the place is a mess, so you get angry and take a forceful

breath in. You are going to tell somebody off for leaving it that way, but in a calm and controlled manner, so you breathe out as you leave.

Breathe in, you've just had a brilliant idea! Then you realize it isn't that great, so you breathe out again. Oh! You've had another idea, so breathe in again – but no, that's not such a good idea either, and you breathe out again.

You are sitting on a park bench enjoying the peace and tranquillity of your surroundings, and you breathe out slowly. Then someone comes and sits down next to you and they smell repugnant. You breathe in as the shock of the smell is overwhelming. You let that breath out and then hold it so you don't inhale any more smell. The person finally leaves the bench and you breathe out again.

Make up your own scenarios and experiment with other ways that you can use breath to add to the action or emotion within a scene.

BREATH WITH OBJECTS

Breath can also be used in relation to objects. When you lift a heavy weight you tend to breathe in when you lift it up, and breathe out when you put it down. It's the same with pushing and pulling: you breathe out when you push, and breathe in when you pull. You might want to start paying attention to your breath in everyday life so you can see what happens to your breath when moving around and doing different things. This will help you figure out how to add it to your mime work.

Pushing

1. Stand up straight and imagine you are going to push a heavy object that is in front of you.
2. You start pushing at it, so you breathe out.
3. When you stop, breathe in.

Pulling

1. You are going to start pulling a rope.
2. Pull the rope towards you and breathe in.
3. When you stop pulling, breathe out.

We usually take our breath for granted. Our breathing is connected to our emotions, and this is why an audience will empathize with your character in a performance when you consciously use breath to have an effect. Everyone has a subconscious understanding of breath because we all experience our own breathing patterns in emotional situations.

Breath is also very involved with exertion, and can be used in mime to give more credibility to movements that involve strength.

6
THE LEVELS OF TENSION

Sometimes there is a lack of connection between a character's situation and the body tension of the actor portraying them. Actors can be in a scene where they are supposed to be in a dangerous situation, yet their performance is not truly believed because their body tension is telling the audience that things are not as bad for them as we are being asked to imagine.

Lecoq taught about the seven levels of tension. Over time I have altered these principles as other teachers have, but here we will look at the basics of the exercise. These different levels of physical tension are great ways to perform different physical states.

THE STATES OF TENSION

Level 1: Comatose

Your body is lying on the ground and you can barely move. Imagine that you are in the desert looking for water, and you haven't had any for ages. You are crawling on the ground trying to push up on to your arms, but you keep falling back down flat on your face.

Level 2: Barely Standing

At this level, you manage to push yourself off the ground and half stand up. You can take a few steps, but have to stop before you can start walking slowly again.

Level 3: Economic

You now have enough energy to walk normally and stand up straight. You save energy by becoming very efficient in your movements. All your actions are economic, precise and concise. You only do what you have to do, and nothing else.

1. Comatose: lying on the ground.

2. 'Barely standing': struggling to stay on your feet.

3. 'Level of economy': walking around efficiently.

Level 4: Everyday

In this level you are back to your usual self, and you can walk around as you do in everyday life. You don't have to conserve energy, but neither do you expend extra energy. You can walk around freely and engage in the world, but you don't have any actions that are elevated by emotion.

Level 5: Curiosity

You are now at a level of tension that is heightened by the things around you. You have an extra spring in your step, and you move lightly and quickly from one thing to another with the curiosity of a child.

5. 'Curiosity': moving with light and quick movements.

Level 6: Fire

Here there is a real sense of urgency: everything is fight or flight! This level has the same rhythm as the fire element. You could be late for a very important job interview, or you are excited about going

6. 'Fire': high energy, and erratic movements.

on a date with the love of your life. You are running around from one thing to the next.

Level 7: *Rigor Mortis*

The opposite of being comatose. The level of tension in your body is so high that you can't move.

4. 'Every day': walking around as normal.

7. 'Rigor mortis': extreme body tension.

For instance, the love of your life has just come into the room and you hold your breath, scared and unable to move because your whole body has seized up. Or you stand to attention worried about what the drill sergeant will say about your uniform. Or you are the manager of a restaurant and the kitchen is in a mess, and the health inspector has just arrived so you freeze in fear.

EXERCISES TO EXPLORE THE LEVELS OF TENSION

Level 1: Comatose

Begin by lying face down on the ground. Imagine you are on holiday and you've had a great night out in a foreign nightclub. You slowly push yourself up on to your elbows. You're so hung over and tired you collapse back to the floor again. Slowly push up on to your elbows again and look around. You realize you are still in the nightclub, but everyone else has gone! You collapse back on to the floor. With effort you push back up on to your elbows, then on to your hands. The thought of being locked in a nightclub is a bit scary, so you muster some more energy and push yourself on to your knees and slowly begin to stand.

Level 2: Barely Standing

With a bent back, sluggishly take some steps and walk around the room looking for the exit. Your arm movements are heavy and slow, and everything is an effort for you. Go over to the bar in the nightclub and pour yourself a glass of water, which gives you a little refreshment and more energy.

Level 3: Economic

You are feeling much better now and able to function a bit more normally. Walk very carefully around the nightclub still looking for the way out. You check all the doors, but they are all locked. You realize that you may be stuck in here for at least another day, and you start to see the funny side of the situation.

Level 4: Everyday

You laugh to yourself about the situation, which makes you feel more like your normal self. You become rational about the situation, and start to believe that everything will work itself out. There is always a simple solution to any problem. You can simply call for help from your mobile phone! But you see that your phone battery is dead. You continue walking around the room looking for a way out, but can't find one. Things are getting to look quite serious, and you are starting to feel rather worried.

Level 5: Curiosity

All your senses become alert and your eyes start to dart around the room whilst you take quick steps

and try to force open the locked doors. You smell gas in the air and think there must be a gas leak, and the gas is slowly beginning to fill the room.

Level 6: Fire

You start to panic and run quickly around the room, desperately trying to find something to break through the doors. You shout for help, but

as you do, you breathe in more gas. The gas leak gets loud, and you are terrified that something is about to explode.

Level 7: *Rigor Mortis*

Something goes bang very loudly! You think the gas has just created an explosion. You freeze, utterly still. You are so petrified, you think you are about to die and you are stuck to the spot. But suddenly the main doors of the club burst open: the fire brigade has arrived, and the firemen turn off the gas. You let out a huge sigh of relief and collapse on to the floor.

Using levels of tension in a sequential order is a way of telling a story, but play around with them. Go from Level 7 to Level 1. Mix them around in order. Explore them, and see how many ways you can use them in different scenarios. Imagine you are a soldier nearly asleep in bed at your army barracks, and then you realize you are supposed to be on duty. Throw yourself out of bed immediately, and then freeze, thinking how much trouble you are going to be in. This little idea could be played by going through all the levels in order at great speed.

Some actors find the right level of tension naturally without even knowing about the different levels. If you can do this, or know about them already, they are still a great tool to be aware of so that you can fine-tune your performance when you need inspiration. For example, to convey a high level of urgency, operate at Level 6; for a character with light and curious qualities, play at Level 5 – and so on.

7
MIME ILLUSIONS

THE MOONWALK

The Moonwalk was made famous by Michael Jackson's film *The Moonwalker*. In actual fact it is the wrong term for this move: it is really called the 'Back Slide,' because that's exactly what you do with your feet – you slide each foot backwards keeping the heel on the floor. A real mime 'Moonwalk' means moving very slowly with big strides and overlarge, smooth movements, as if you were walking on the moon! However, we'll continue to call the Michael Jackson moves the 'Moonwalk', as this is its most recognized name.

Doing the Moonwalk

1. Stand up straight, arms by your sides with your feet parallel and close together.
2. Keep your right leg straight with the right foot flat on the ground. Bend the left leg so your left foot is raised but the toes are still touching the floor.
3. On the spot, change leg positions so your left leg is straight with the left foot flat on the floor, and the right leg is bent with the right heel raised and the toes still on the floor. Keep swapping the positions from leg to leg on the spot. Make sure your toes on the foot with the bent leg are always touching the floor. Once you are used to this motion, it's time to add the back slide.
4. With your bent leg, push down through the toes until your heel is flat on the ground. This leg takes all the weight. At the same time, slide your straight leg backwards, keeping your heel very close to the floor, so your foot maintains

Ready position, standing straight.

Right leg straight, left leg bent.

a horizontal position all the way through the movement. Keep your leg straight as it moves backwards. Don't go back too far with your foot, just a few inches will be enough. Going back further will make things harder for yourself.
5. Now keeping your feet where they are, bend your right knee and straighten your left knee so you have swapped the position of your legs. Your back leg is now bent with the toes on the ground, and the front leg is straight with a flat heel.
6. Transfer all the weight on to your back foot and do the same again: slide your front leg backwards a few inches (keep your leg straight and the heel close to the floor). Stop and swap legs again, and continue the moves until you

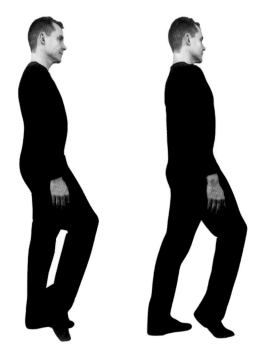

Left leg straight, right leg bent.

Slide the straight leg backwards.

Swap legs.

feel confident of them. It's important to transfer your weight from one foot to the other and then make the slide backwards.

Once you are confident with it, try to get to the point where there isn't the obvious pause in the middle of steps so it all looks like a single, continuous movement. You will now be walking the Moonwalk!

You can also add in the arm movement. The arms should move in opposition to your legs, so as the left leg moves backwards, your right arm will swing forwards, and vice versa. This can be tricky to get right, so I would recommend adding the arms once you have mastered the Moonwalk so you don't have to think about what your legs are doing.

Having mastered the Moonwalk, you could mime a wall beside you, so you create the illusion that you are pushing yourself backwards. You can try another trick with an actual prop such as an umbrella. Imagine that it is a really stormy day and the wind is pushing you backwards. Throw your arms backwards with the umbrella in one hand, and push forwards from the chest and the head. Do the Moonwalk on the spot to show the strength of the wind.

THE WALL

The Wall is the classic mime routine, commonly used as 'The Wall' and 'Trapped in a Glass Box'. These are the mime illusions that many people associate with the stereotypical mime artist.

Doing the Mime Wall doesn't make you a great mime artist, but it does seem to be the illusion to have under your belt for people to think that you are. It's a fun trick that is often requested by students. So here are the steps to learn the Mime Wall for yourself.

The Mime Wall

1. Stand up straight, your arms by your sides; ensure that your arms and hands are relaxed.

Lift your right hand up in front of you with your palm facing out and just below shoulder height. Make sure there is no tension in your hand – remember that tension makes it look as if you are already holding something.

2. In mime, there is usually a reverse movement to articulate an action. So, move your right arm backwards about an inch, then move it forwards to put your hand on the wall.

3. Just as you place your hand on the wall, tense the hand so your fingers are spread out like the toes of a gecko. Make sure your hand is completely straight and vertical, and not slanting forwards or backwards or on any angle.

4. Leave your right hand where it is in fixed space, and do the same thing with your left hand. Bring it up in front of you, just below shoulder height. Move it backwards about an inch, and then move your hand forwards on to the wall.

5. Tense your hand, and spread your fingers as it hits the surface. Imagine your hand is a blob of paint that has been thrown against a wall and it splats all over it. That tiny explosion effect is what you are looking to reproduce.

6. You now have both hands on the wall. Take your right hand away from the wall, relax it as you do, and bring it back an inch. Keeping your right hand in a vertical position, drop it down, about a hand span length. Then put it back on the wall, tensing the hand as before when you make contact with the invisible surface.

Relax the right hand.

The left hand moves towards the wall.

Place the right hand on the wall.

Both hands are tense on the wall.

Place the right hand below on the wall.

Place the left hand next to the right hand.

Relax the left hand.

7. At this point your right hand is lower than the left hand, so bring the left hand down in line with the right hand in the same way. Relax the left hand off the wall.
8. Place your left hand parallel to the right hand, and place it back on the wall whilst tensing your hand and fingers. Repeat the exercise from the beginning so that you are tracing your hands in a square, hitting the same four spots on the wall.

Remember to move only one hand at a time, otherwise the effect will look messy. All you are really doing are two key movements with the hands:

tense, relax, tense, relax and so on, whilst moving your arm positions.

Once you have this really solid, speed it up and then focus on the hand technique of tense and relax.

Other Things

Place both hands on the wall in front of you. Leaving your hands and feet where they are, lean left and right and try to keep your hands fixed in the air. A little trick to add to the illusion further is that as you lean to the right, slightly push your hands to the left. When you lean to the right, push your hands to the left.

Try moving your hands in different positions on the wall: turn your hands to the side so your fingers are pointing to the right or left, or point one hand up and the other hand to the side. Find the corner of the wall and put both hands around the side of it at a 90-degree angle to look round the corner.

Play around and experiment how else your hands can be placed on the wall. Turn them upside down, and put them behind you as if you have your back to the wall and are walking along a very narrow ledge.

TRAPPED IN A GLASS BOX

Being trapped in a glass box really doesn't need much explanation. A mime artist is stuck in a glass box and is looking for a way out of it. The basics are very simple and it's easy to learn. Making it look good is just down to practice.

1. Stand up straight and place both hands in front of you, at shoulder height, fingers pointing up and with tension. You are trapped in a glass box the size of an old telephone booth. There are four equal sides to the glass box, and you are going to move round it in a clockwise direction.
2. Turn your head 90 degrees to the right.
3. Relax your right hand off the glass wall in front of you, and now place it on the glass wall, where your head is looking, 90 degrees to your right. Remember to make tension in the hand as it hits the surface, as you learnt in 'The Wall' exercise.
4. Leaving both hands where they are (the left hand is on the front glass wall, the right hand

2. Turn your head to your right.

1. Start with both hands on the wall.

3. Place your right hand on the right wall.

is on the right glass wall), turn your body 90 degrees to face the right side of the wall. Some people get their feet muddled up here and one leg seems to get left behind. So make it easy for yourself. When you turn 90 degrees on the spot, transfer all your weight to your left foot, so you can turn your right foot to face the right glass wall as well. Once you have done that, transfer your weight to your right foot and bring your left foot parallel to your right foot. Both feet will now be facing the right glass wall.

5. The last move is to bring your left hand over to the right side, parallel to your right hand. Remember to relax it coming away from the wall, and to tense it as it makes contact again.

That's it! Five easy moves to create a 'glass box'.

Now repeat the movements, always turning to your right so you end up back in the direction you started from. Then do it all anti-clockwise, turning to the left.

5. Place the left hand on the right wall.

Master it all, then start to have fun with it! See how fast or how slowly you can move round the box, always being mindful to move only one part of your body at a time. Don't let the illusion get boring for you or your audience. Tell the story of someone trapped in a glass box, they might be trying to escape; it's important to keep the technique interesting. Place one hand on the ceiling, try and push a wall and look for a trap door. Then find a way out. Get your audience engaged in story and not technique. They shouldn't really even see your technique if the story-telling is good enough. Remember that the technique is only there to help you create a story. A great story added to great technique would be ideal, but stories are the heartbeat of what makes us human.

PULLING THE ROPE

When creating the effect of pushing or pulling mimed objects, we need to see a real exertion of

4. Turn your body to the right.

effort. If you fake this, the action becomes fake, and people hate fakes. A mime must be completely and physically engaged in the actions they make. This is not to be confused with 'method acting', as there is no real emotion to be found in mime. If you are pushing a mime wall, you need to have the same physical commitment that you would have in pushing a real wall.

Pulling a rope in mime is a very useful illusion to practise because you can transfer the mechanics of this motion to a gesture.

1. Bend down and pick up an imaginary rope, keeping your hands relaxed as you move them towards the rope, then tense them as you grab it. The left hand grabs the rope from underneath and the right hand grabs the rope on top.
2. Make sure you don't make a fist with your hands: if you do, the rope will look like it's as thin as a thread. Instead make a circle with your thumb and index finger, while the other fingers bunch tightly together, completing the circle. Imagine that you are going to pull the rope from your left side to your right side.
3. Turn to face the direction of the rope and pull it backwards along your right side. As you pull, move into a backward lunge. Your left leg is straight with the foot flat on the ground, and your right leg is bent. Raise your

2. Make a circle grip with your hands.

3. Move into a backward lunge.

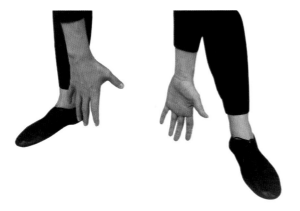

1. Bend down and pick up the rope.

right heel so that all your weight is on your toes.
4. You should be in a position where you have pulled the rope as far backwards to your right as possible. Let go of it by relaxing and unclasping your right hand. This is a 'letting go' action.

4. Let go of the rope with your right hand.

6. Let go of the rope with your left hand.

5. Reach for the rope with your right hand.

7. Move into a forward lunge position.

5. Reach out in an arc shape, moving your right hand over your head to where the rope would be in front of you, and tense your hand as you grasp it again.

6. Keeping your right hand where it is, let go of the rope with your left hand.

7. Move into a forward lunge position, as you reach for the rope with your left hand. Once

you have got the hang of this, these two moves need to happen at the same time.

8. Grab the rope with your left hand.
9. Pull the rope backwards again along your right side and move into a backward lunge at the same time. Make sure you don't go into a standing position when you are pulling the rope backwards. Keep your height low and even all the way through this movement. Otherwise it will look rather odd. You are then ready to repeat the sequence.

Pulling the rope is actually only three moves: reach with the right hand, reach with the left hand, then pull backwards and repeat.

Try pulling the rope in other ways. You could turn your back on the rope, then begin in a forward lunge position and try to pull it that way. Imagine you own a ship and you are pulling in a heavy anchor. You could sit on the floor and pull it up very slowly that way. We must see the heavy resistance in your body when you are pulling. You have to genuinely exert yourself and pull – it has to be hard work otherwise the audience won't believe that the

9. Move into a backward lunge position.

thing you are pulling is heavy. Everyone has pushed and pulled something heavy, so we notice the truth in your actions. When you do this exercise properly you will know it because you will be exhausted and will have developed your thigh muscles by balancing all your weight on your backward lunge.

CLIMBING A LADDER

How does a mime climb a ladder? It's all about making the illusion simple and effective. It's a trick that a lot of people enjoy watching.

1. Stand up straight. Put your right hand up at shoulder height and grab a ladder rung: tense your hand first, then make a circle with your thumb and index finger. The rest of the fingers curl around to complete the circle (in the same way as grabbing the rope). You have just grabbed one of the rungs of the ladder.
2. Do the same with your left hand but at the level of your waist, so your left arm is making a 90-degree angle.

8. Grab the rope with your left hand.

1. Grab the ladder with your right hand.

3. Place your right leg on the ladder.

2. Grab the ladder with your left hand.

3. You now have both hands on the ladder. You are ready to start climbing. Bend your right knee so you have elevated your right leg. You are making a 90-degree angle at your hip, knee and foot joint. This foot angle means you have placed one foot on the step of the ladder.

4. To climb the ladder, bend your left leg keeping the rest of your body, arms and right leg still. As your left knee bends and your whole body gets closer to the ground, follow the movement with your bent right leg until your right foot makes contact with the floor. You should

4. Lower yourself to a squatting position.

now be in a squatting position with your weight spread evenly between both feet. Keep your back straight in your squat.

5. Let go of the ladder with your left hand (don't forget to tense, then relax) and grab another rung above your right hand by tensing and grabbing.

6. Straighten your right leg, keep your left knee bent as you rise from your squatting position and create the 90-degree angle with your hip, knee and foot joints on your left-hand side. Imagine the left knee has been glued in that bent position. As you straighten your right leg, keep both hands in fixed space. It can help the illusion if you move both hands down a fraction at the same time as your leg straightens.

7. Bend your right leg to lower your whole body as before. Keep your hands in the same place, and lower the left leg in time with the right leg bend until your left foot touches the floor.

6. Straighten your right leg.

5. Grab the next rung of the ladder with your left hand.

7. Bend your right leg to a squatting position.

9. Place both hands on top of the ladder.

8. To continue climbing, grab the next rung with your right hand so your left leg will now straighten, and lift the body again so you make the 90-degree angle with your right leg.

10. Push the ladder down with your bent leg.

11. Push the ladder towards the ground.

9. To get to the top of the ladder, place both hands on the same rung.
10. Push the ladder down with your bent leg and push down with your hands at the same time.
11. Lift up the other leg, put it on the ladder rung, and push it down further towards the ground, as before.
12. Keep doing this until you can place one foot between your hands.

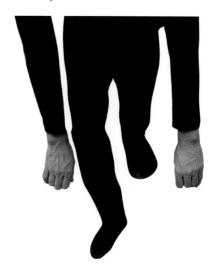

12. Place your foot between your hands.

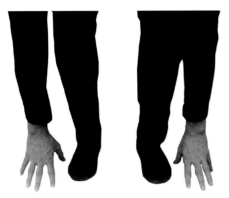

Push the ladder into the floor.

13. Finally, push both your hands and leg into the floor. You are now at the top of the ladder.

As you go up or down the ladder, try to keep the same distance between the placement of your feet and hands on the rungs.

Other Things

If you wanted to mime climbing a rock face, you can use the same technique. The only difference is that your hands don't have to be in line with each other, and they will make a cup shape around the rocks instead of circles for the straight ladder rungs. It is useful to watch yourself in the mirror or to film yourself with a phone so you can keep a check on body alignment and posture.

PUSHING AGAINST A WALL

Pushing against a wall is one of the most useful illusions to learn in mime. If you can do the pushing illusion, you can apply it to real objects so that it looks as if things are stuck in the air (fixed space) and people become awestruck. It looks as if you are defying the laws of physics, and most people want to learn how to do it after seeing it performed. It's like watching a magician make a card disappear. The mime of pushing against the wall uses the opposite movements of pulling a rope. It's good to use when performing 'Trapped in a Glass Box' and pushing mime or real objects of all sizes.

1. As a warm-up to this exercise, stand up straight and walk over to a real wall.
2. Thrust your hips forwards, keeping your back straight. Push really hard to see if you can move the wall. You should notice that you are in a forward lunge position – your back leg is straight with the foot flat on the ground with your front leg bent. There is little to no weight placed on the front foot. Notice where the tension is in your body. If you push really hard, you will notice that your head and chest push forwards too.
3. In mime we have to reproduce that truth. So recreate your position without pushing on the wall. Step into a forward lunge position, back leg straight, foot flat and front leg bent. Lift your heel and put your weight on your toes. We move away from the truth of the action now to enhance the appearance of the illusion. Again this mime will strengthen your thighs!

    Move both hands up in front of you, hands flat and vertical, your fingers spread with tension and ready to put on the wall at shoulder height.

Push a wall.

Forward lunge position.

we are pushing with force and that all our weight is being used to push against the wall. To do this, we have to make it seem that there is no weight on our front foot, so we bend our front leg, lift our heel and put the weight on our toes. This is hard work!

4. Make sure your back is straight. Pushing your hips forwards will help to straighten your back. Move back about an inch from the wall, and your hands will be fixed in the air (fixed space). They will stay in this position when you start to mime pushing the wall.

5. Push your head and chest forwards at the same time. We have to create the illusion that

6. Stop pushing into the wall, and move back an inch by letting your front heel touch down on to the floor. As you do this keep your hands in the same place (fixed space). You are having a quick rest before you start to push the wall again. Start pushing the wall again by lifting your heel and putting your weight on to your toes again.

7. Repeat several times making sure that your back is straight and your chest and head are pushed forwards. Once you've done that, swivel your front knee left to right. This also helps to give the illusion that there is no weight on your front leg. Now go back to a real wall and try pushing it again. You will notice that you can easily swivel your front leg from side to side. Move back an inch again and practise the mime version of pushing the wall again. Use the real wall to test out what you are doing, and move away again, back into the mime of it. You want to get so good

Mime pushing, one inch away from a real wall.

Resting position.

at it that someone watching can't tell the difference between whether you are pushing at a wall or not. In performance, it's always best to do this illusion on a side profile so the audience can see the whole length of your forward lunge.

You can use this routine using real objects, too. Try pushing an empty plastic water bottle, a balloon or a hat. They can appear to have a life of their own, they look as if they are stuck in the air and won't move. The real object that you are going to push has to be light in weight, otherwise it will be too heavy for you to keep fixed in the air as you move around it.

To push an object forwards in space just roll one side of your chest forwards, and straight afterwards, push the object in front of you about twelve inches. Stop, keep the object still (fixed space), switch legs and do the same again.

Use the forward lunge as a gesture. Instead of pushing an object or a wall, pretend you are saying 'no' to someone, and lunge forwards as the gesture. When we say 'no', we push something away, so this matches with physically pushing away as well.

WALKING THE DOG

The best mime illusions are the ones that let the audience imagine what is actually being mimed. 'Walking the Dog' is a great example of this. When you see this being performed you should be able to see in your mind's eye what kind of dog it is, its personality, its shape and its size.

Imagine you are walking a dog in the park, but it has a mind of its own and you can't control which direction it goes in.

1. Stand up straight and hold a mime dog lead with a very enthusiastic and excited dog standing next to you.
2. Bend down and pat the dog. Stroke the dog from head to tail, by curving your hand down

and then flat to show the length of the dog. Do this a couple of times to show the audience what kind of a dog you have. Maybe it has long floppy ears, or it's very tiny. As the dog is very excitable and panting very quickly, you will have to show this with your facial expressions. You have to mirror what the dog is like. So maybe your head is nodding up and down slightly as you stroke the dog, your mouth is in an open smile, and you breathe a small panting breath yourself. Stand up and walk around the room imagining you are in a park.

3. As you start to walk, let your hand be pulled in front of you as if the dog is straining against the lead in one definite direction.
4. Suddenly the dog changes direction and pulls you quickly over to the right to sniff a tree. Let your hand be pulled even further and to your right side. The hand leads the action and pulls your elbow, which pulls your shoulder, which pulls your body, and finally your head, which falls back with the surprise of the pull. The key here is that your head is the last thing that moves. The sequence is hand – elbow – shoulders – body – head. Practise this a number of times, breaking down each movement one at a time. Try it in slow motion first, so you can speed it up later.

Stroke the dog.

Arm stretches out.

Your hand pulls the arm forwards.

5. Once you have mastered this series of isolated movements in order, start to play around with different rhythms. The dog can pull you in many different directions, and can change every few seconds. It's as if your arm and body are being whipped around like the carriages of

a rollercoaster. Let your hand pull you – it's as if it has a life of its own and you can't control it.

Make up a story about walking the dog: for example, the dog gets worn out and finally takes a rest. You tell it off and it runs off again, taking you with it. I like to pull the dog back to me to end the story, using the 'Pulling the Rope' mime exercise.

THE DOOR

At some time or another you are going to need to mime a door, either to get out of a glass box or because there isn't a real door in your set. It sounds such a simple mime, but when most people do it for the first time, their door is light as air and the door handle is as thin as a needle. This exercise will help you open and close a pretend door with a touch of credibility.

1. From standing, place both hands on to the door at shoulder height, in the same way you would with the wall mime.
2. Keeping your left hand still, make an outward circular movement with your right hand, towards the door handle, which is underneath your left elbow.
3. Now grab the door handle and make the same shape with your hand as you do when climbing a ladder or pulling the rope: thumb and

1. Place both hands on the door.

2. The right hand circles outwards.

4. Turn your body 90 degrees to your left.

index finger touching to make a circle, with the rest of your fingers bunched tightly together to complete the circle.

4. Turn your body 90 degrees to your left, keeping your hands in fixed space. Your feet are parallel to each other now, and facing to the left from your original position.

5. To prepare to open the door, move a fraction away from it, and then try to push it open. Turn the handle on the door using your wrist only. The door will not budge. You can push your

head and chest in front of you as you do when pushing the wall to open the door in a mime performance.

6. Repeat. Relax back away from the door and push it: again the door won't budge. So you keep trying to push the door open.

7. Go with the 'Rule of Three', and try the door again. This time the door opens. The 'Rule of Three' consists of two unsuccessful repeat

3. Grabbing the door handle.

5. Backing away from the door.

6. Pushing forwards to open the door.

7–8. Swing the door open 90 degrees.

moves/actions/sentences/words that set up the action, then a successful attempt. Here we have two attempts to open the door, and on the third try we get it open.

8. As the door opens, keep your hands in the same position and turn your body 90 degrees on the spot to your right. Your hands follow the line of movement that your body makes.

9. Before you walk through the doorway, tense both hands wide open, then relax them and bring them away from the door.

10. Walk through and turn around 180 degrees to close the door behind you. To do this, use your left hand to grab the door handle. With a re-laxed hand, go towards the handle, then tense your hand as you grab it. Move into a forward lunge, and swing the door in an arc to close it. End the action with 'toc' (a short, sharp move-ment). This will complete and add a full stop to the door being closed.

11. Repeat and practise to perfect your mime door technique.

Try using the door mime as part of the story in the 'glass box' exercise. Think of other stories you can

8–9. Tense the hands to release the door.

use the door mime in, so you can practise your technique and story-telling skills. Maybe you've walked into the wrong (unlocked) hotel room – you see the occupant in there, feel embarrassed, and close the door behind you. Then you open it again because you can't believe your own eyes and you want to have another look!

10. Move into a forward lunge to close the door.

THE PUNT

The punt is the classic boat ride in Venice (or Cambridge) where the punter uses a long pole to push the boat along the river. The exercise starts off being about a real-life experience, but can shift to become something more abstract and metaphysical.

The Punt Exercise

1. Imagine you are standing on a boat in Venice with a very long pole. Stand with your legs wide apart with your left leg bent and your right leg straight. Hold the pole (circle grip with the thumb and index finger) with your hands in a diagonal position: your right hand holds the pole high up in the air above your right shoulder, and the left hand holds the pole about waist height.
2. Push the pole downwards into the water on your left side – at the same time your right leg bends and your left straightens. Keep pushing the pole until your arms naturally move to

1. Wide stance, ready position.

2. Pushing the pole forwards.

as far as they can comfortably go. Keep the same distance between your hands as you move them.

3. From this position bring the pole back in front of you by moving your left hand closer to the centre of your body and with the right hand doing the same, so the right is above the left and your legs are now both bent at the knee.

4. Keep the movement flowing to the right side while keeping the hands the same distance apart until your right leg is bent again.

5. Now we are going to change our hand grip. With your left hand let go of the pole below.

6. Now place your left hand a few inches away above your right hand and grip the top of the pole. Your left palm should be facing downwards and be in a wide claw shape.

7. Let go of the pole with your right hand and place it on top of the left hand.

8. Now we push the pole deeper into the water. Using the push technique described in 'The Wall' exercise, push the pole into the water a few inches. The pole won't go any further, so you have to push it a second time and now it moves deeper into the water. Really

4. Moving the pole across to your right side.

stretch into the lunge, let go with your right hand and keep pushing with your left hand deeper into the water. Your right arm can move behind your body to give you some counterbalance.

3. Bring the pole in front of your body.

5. Letting go of the pole with your left hand.

6. Place the left hand on top of the pole.

8. Deep lunge forwards with your left hand.

7. Place the right hand on top of the left hand.

9. Pull the pole back up out of the mud with your left hand, all the way over to your left side above your left shoulder, and move backwards into a left-sided lunge. Bring your right arm in front of you again. This is another counterbalance, which completes this move.

10. With your right arm grab the pole at mid-thigh level and pull it upwards, across your body, on a diagonal line towards your left shoulder. As you do this, let go of the pole with your left hand and let it naturally fall down to your side.

11. With your left hand now free, move it in front of and across your body to the right side, and grab the pole at waist height. Don't let go of the pole with your right hand, just keep it where it is for now. If you are doing this correctly, you will find that your arms are crossed over each other now.

12. Finally, move both hands back to your original position with your left leg bent.

9. Pull the pole out of the water.

10. The right hand pulls the pole across to the left.

12. Move back to the original starting position.

13. Repeat the steps several times, until you can do them all together without thinking about them. It will take some time to settle into it, but it will be easy enough when you do.

This exercise can be used to teach mime on many levels.

Level 1 – Technique: This level is the simple mime technique, as above.

Level 2 – Breath: Connect the breath to each movement – for example, every time you push the pole, breathe out, and when you pull it, breathe in.

Level 3 – Resonance: Playing with a slow pace of movement gives the sequence a poetic quality. You give the actions a mystical quality so it's not so technical.

11. The left hand grabs the pole at waist height.

Level 4 – Pleasure: When you are performing the punt, the mime must convey a sense of pleasure in doing the movements so that he/she conveys that joy and as a result gives it to the audience.

Level 5 – Gesture: This is where the mime technique blurs and the hands become relaxed with less technique used. The movement becomes more abstract, and it can look as if we are pushing someone away or trying to pull someone or something towards us. The motion becomes more like Tai Chi, with soft hands, the breath and resonance performed with pleasure.

Level 6 – Spiritual: Here the essence of the punt movements remain, but they have now become so abstract that we are now working on a deeper level. The external movement now relates to the internal feelings of the person. The story is no longer literal, it has become profound, and that has a more spiritual place.

THE ROBOT

The Robot dance is always one that is performed badly in night clubs! I learnt to move like a robot in my breakdance days. One day I got a call to work on the film *The Avengers: Age of Ultron*. It was motion capture work, so I wore a motion capture suit so my movements could be recorded for Ultron, the big, bad CGI robot character. I did different scenes moving in lots of different ways. It was a lot of fun and the team were brilliant to work with. The Robot is handy to know, not just because you might get called to do a film, but because it's useful to know about mechanical movement. The Robot moves its body parts in isolation from each other, one move at a time, and can do so at speed or slowly.

The Robot Exercise

1. Stand up straight with both arms raised at 90 degrees in front of you. Make sure your hands and fingers are straight and your fingers are tightly bunched together.
2. The key thing to remember with the robot is that there is always a backward movement before a forward movement. So to raise both arms upwards from the elbows, you have to move them downwards first, with a quick, short, sharp toc movement.
3. Then slowly and smoothly move your arms upwards and stop abruptly as if they just locked into place.
4. To move the arms back down again, do the same thing in reverse. Move the arms upwards first with a short sharp toc movement, then slowly and smoothly move them down. Bring the movement to an abrupt stop as they lock into place.
5. Let's try some head movements. To turn your head to your right, you have to do a toc movement to your left first. Then slowly and smoothly turn the head to the right and stop it suddenly, like a full stop. Try the same thing to your left side.
6. To turn your torso left or right, do exactly the same thing. To turn the torso to the right, do a toc towards your left side first, followed by the liquid, smooth movement to your right. Toc and stop.
7. Using this simple principle, try it out with other parts of your body. Use the same technique when turning your wrists around. Open and close your hands in the same way, keeping your fingers together as you do it. Try different combinations of movement – for example look left, turn the torso left, turn the wrists around.
8. You can walk as a robot in two ways. The first is to keep your legs straight and your feet flat, and shuffle forwards with small steps. The second is to do this in a slow-moving mechanical way. Take a step forwards into a small lunge, keeping your body in line with the lunge. Your body will be on a 45-degree angle. Push backwards with your front leg so you are in an upright position again. Now repeat this with the other leg: slide your back leg forwards, keeping

the heel close to the ground, and move into a small forward lunge. Your body is in a straight line with your back leg. Then push backwards on your front leg.

9. Now it is time to mix it up and try different body isolations and combinations to see how you can make your robot come alive. Keep your facial expression neutral or expressionless as you do.

Remember the robot is made of metal or a hard plastic. As it is man-made you want to try and demonstrate this inhuman effect by using the backward movements.

What happens when your robot breaks down and starts malfunctioning? When it finally comes to a complete stop? And after a moment it reactivates again?

If you observe factory machines with hydraulics you will notice the smoothness in the movement. Remember this smoothness when you move from one point to another. If you want to make the robot more like an android (as C3P0 from *Star Wars*), use more fixed points and make your arm and head movements stiff. All the backward movements should be nearly invisible, so keep that thought in the back of your mind because it will add a little stutter to your movement. Once you understand the basic mechanics of the movements, you can play around with them and invent your own style of robotics.

THE PUPPET

The Thunderbirds theatre show in the West End, performed a number of years ago, had two actors performing as 'real' puppets, like the marionettes from the original television series. They were brilliant. What I liked most of all was that they had spent considerable time on their performance so they could emulate how puppets really move. They were wonderful and credible. To perform as a puppet you use body isolations with a lightness of movement (the air element). It's a lot harder to do than the robot, as it is very exhausting!

The Puppet Exercise

1. Move into a deep sitting position from standing.
2. Put both your arms in front of you at a 90-degree angle, with your wrists relaxed and your back and head straight. Relax your shoulders. Imagine that you are suspended by strings that are attached to your hands, back, head and knees.
3. Maintaining this position, move your body, arms and head up and down slightly – and I mean ever so slightly – to show that the puppeteer has just picked up your strings and is about to move you.
4. Start with the head first. Move your head from left to right, and as you do, think of those bobbing toy dogs that you see in the back of a car. Keep the bobbing very light and small. If your movements get too big, your puppet will be unrealistic.
5. As you move your head to the left, move both your arms to the right, with the small, light bobbing movement described above. Bob your head to the right and bob your arms to the left. Your head and arms are not connected to each other, and there isn't the precision that the robot has.
6. Try walking as a puppet. To do this you must be in a deep sitting position with both arms at 90 degrees in front of you. To move your right leg forwards, the step begins from the right knee, so transfer all your weight to your left leg. Bring the right knee up and keep the foot flat, as if it is still on the floor. Pull up from your back as you take a step, and keep your back and head straight.
7. When you put your right foot back on the floor, sink into a deep sitting position. Stop for a second or two and have a brief moment bobbing up and down with your arms and your head. It will keep the lightness and movement of the puppet alive before you take your next step.
8. Take another step with your left leg in the same way.

9. Practise walking around the room. Remember that the head and arms are always slightly bobbing even when the puppet comes to a stop. The only time the puppet doesn't move is when the puppeteer has hung you up, or if he has let go of the strings, when you would have to collapse on the floor in a heap.

10. Practise moving one arm at a time up and down. As you do this keep your hands relaxed – they never have any tension in them. Practise moving one leg at a time with a longer pause in the middle before the next step. Try performing simple tasks such as waving. Could a puppet mime the glass box?

You can have a lot of fun with the puppet, although at the beginning it's going to be a lot of hard work because you are in a deep seated position for most of the time. It also takes effort to keep the constant bobbing going all the time, especially when you are walking, with your head turning in one direction and your arms in the other. With lots of practice, when you get it right it will look amazing. Try making up a story when the puppet takes off its strings and comes to life, like Pinocchio.

SLOW MOTION

I was also hired to be a slow-motion expert for *Sweeney Todd*. It sounds really glamorous, but in reality it was me filming at Shepperton Studios early in the morning in a green screen studio the size of an aircraft hangar. They wanted to film me walking in slow motion: I had to take two steps every 4.8 seconds. That would have been fine if I had had a stopwatch in front of me and could see how much time I had between every step.

This was actually the least of my problems. I had to walk in high-heeled boots, wearing a top hat and long coat with a walking stick. Walking that slowly in heels and using a walking stick is incredibly hard to do while only taking two steps every 4.8 seconds. The film crew were pressed for time, and each time I did the shot, they had to

cut and reshoot it because I looked rather wobbly when I walked. They wanted to speed up the shot later on so that it looked as if I was walking in real time. In the end, I don't think it made the final edit!

To do slow motion really well takes a lot of practice, but when it *is* done well it can have a very dramatic effect. Using slow motion in mime is very useful to highlight a moment in mime. An example of this would be in a running race (going over the finish line), in a fight scene (at the moment of impact), when a bomb is about to explode, or when an astronaut is walking on the moon (the real 'moon walk').

The first thing with slow motion is that everything is highly exaggerated and slowed down.

Slow Motion Exercises

RUNNING RACE

Imagine you are in a running race and you are nearing the finish line. It's a close call, because you have an opponent right behind you. Start by moving into a forward lunge with your right foot, and move ultra slowly into the next lunge with your left foot in front. Move your arms in opposition to your legs as you do when you are really running. Take as much time as you want, the slower the better to begin with – you can always speed up as you get used to moving like this. Engage your facial expressions, and make them slow to change and exaggerated. Take more time than you think you need: think the ultra slow motion that you see in those Hollywood films.

FIGHT SCENE

Imagine you are in a fight scene with an opponent, and go to punch them in the face. Slowly take your right arm back to start the action, and move into a forward lunge as you come forwards – stretch your arm movement forwards to punch them. Over-exaggerate this movement – really stretch as far as you can go, and take more time than you think is needed. Remember to exaggerate your facial expressions, too – they must move at the same speed as your body.

As you throw the punch, your opponent dodges you and hits you smack bang in the face. This impact sends you flying backwards. Your face turns to the side, taking the force of their punch. Take your time. Your face becomes distorted from the punch.

Keep the fight going and see what other things you can do. In a slow-motion fight scene always keep two feet firmly on the floor so you have control and balance at all times. It's hard to balance and move in slow motion on one leg, and the slightest speed increase may make you lose your balance, which will instantly destroy the scene.

WALKING ON THE MOON

This exercise is virtually the same as the slow-motion running race. Take big, deep lunges and let your arms move down as your body goes down. As you come up out of the lunge, let both of your arms float upwards. Your head and facial expressions match the speed of your body movements. Again, when you make your lunges, keep both feet firmly on the ground, or at the very least, keep both feet in contact with the ground.

OTHER SCENARIOS

You are sitting in a café drinking coffee. The love of your life walks in and you move in slow motion as your put your coffee down and lift your head up to track their movement around the chairs and tables. Your eyes slowly widen and your jaw drops open. This is a classic scene that you may have seen in the movies or commercials. It would work really well with some music when the person enters the coffee shop.

It's high noon in a Western, and you've got involved in a bar brawl. Draw your gun out to shoot. Move into slow motion as you are about to shoot, but you get shot first which throws you back and on to the floor. You are going to have to lower yourself to the ground slowly, so first bend your legs and use your knees to get lower to the floor. With an outstretched arm placed carefully and slowly on to the ground, slide your body down. You need to be able to keep in contact with the ground in a controlled manner otherwise it will spoil the effect: make it easy for yourself.

FAST FORWARD

Fast forward is where all the actions are speeded up, like being fast forwarded on an old video tape. Fast forward is a lot easier to do than slow motion, but there is an art to making it look good. When I devised a mime show for the Holt Festival, my partner Ellie and I performed a fast-forward action scene in a restaurant, and we filmed our rehearsals so we could gauge its effectiveness. We worked on the scene over and over again and bit by bit so we could capture each action in the scene to make it the best we could.

When you are moving incredibly quickly you have to be very precise with all your movements. They have to become smaller, and brought in towards the body. It helps to have brief moments of fixed points. It's the complete opposite to performing in slow motion, where all action is exaggerated and heightened. However, fast forward works really well when you mix it with slow motion. Let's look at some examples.

Fast Forward Exercises

EATING DINNER

You are in a restaurant and have just been served the main course, and you are really hungry. In fast forward, pick up your knife and fork and lick your lips. Bring your arms in close and tight to your body, and start cutting up your meal. Fast forward works best when you do one thing at a time at speed. For example, cut up your meal, take a bite, chew, use your facial expressions to show us that you like it (or dislike it), and start the sequence again. Quick and concise is the key. Change your facial expressions in a rapid fire of fixed points.

This takes practice to get into the rhythm: imagine you are a little squirrel chewing away at an acorn, and you get the idea.

Fight Scene

You are about to make that first punch. As you do, speed up into fast forward. Make small, tight punches. Do a quick one, two punch, get hit back in the face, which swipes your head to one side, punch again with a quick one, two, and get hit in the stomach. You will have to feel the timing of how long and how far your head moves back when you get hit. You get punched again in the face, which twirls you quickly on the spot and puts you down on to the floor. To do the fall, spin on the spot and spiral down, using your hands to lower yourself on to the ground. A quick spin will help keep the action tight so it works with the effect of doing fast forward.

Late for Work

Lie down on the floor and imagine you are at home in bed, and you slowly wake up. Slowly pick up the clock next to your bed: you realize you have overslept. Make a big physical reaction to this, and start moving in fast-forward mode. Jump in the shower, wash, put on your clothes, grab some food, and hurry out of the house. Hail a bus, jump on board and sit down – and return to normal speed. Take quick breaths looking straight ahead, thinking about how you are going to get in trouble with your boss. Like everything in fast forward, do everything quickly and concisely, and one thing at a time. Don't take too long having a shower – as long as the audience gets the idea, quickly move to getting dressed.

Using Fast Forward

The art is to find the right balance of speed and clarity of movement. Film yourself and watch it to see if it's working or not. Even better, show someone what you are doing, and see if they understand what you are doing without telling them first.

Try doing the fight scene with fast forward mixed with some slow motion. Make transitions from fast to slow, snapping between each pace. Add a pause after the change, and then continue. Play around and see what variations you can come up with. How does changing the pace highlight different parts of the action and the characters' story?

Fast-forward motion is great for showing part of a story again. Try doing your actions in reverse, as when you rewind a videotape. As you practise this, you can start to find ways to show an audience exactly what you are doing and where you are, in as efficient a way as possible so you don't have to repeat actions.

A NEWSPAPER

When my students perform a scene on a train, they usually add an older character reading a newspaper. (It is interesting that we don't associate younger people with reading the newspaper any more – we assume they are texting on their smartphones.)

To mime reading a newspaper is very good practice for body isolations because you mostly use your head. Decroux has a wonderful scenario reading a newspaper, a highly choreographed sequence of movements. The beauty with his newspaper scene is that if you complete each movement correctly, you naturally flow into the next movement. The following exercise is a simple set of movements, but check out the Decroux version on YouTube.

The Newspaper Exercise

1. Stand up straight or sit down on a chair – it won't matter which one you choose as all the movement is in your upper body.
2. You have a large newspaper in both hands and you are about to read it.
3. Bring both hands together in front of you, using what I call the 'OK Grip,' where your

thumb and index finger make a circle and the rest of your fingers are spread. Pinch open the newspaper in front of you.

4. Open it out wide on either side so you are ready to read it.
5. Using your head, not your eyes, show that you are reading the newspaper by moving your head from left to right and moving down the first page, then up to the top of second page, and left to right and down that page.
6. Turn a page with your left hand: relax your hand open and off the page it is holding, move it to the right side of the newspaper and tense/ grab the next page with the 'OK Grip'.
7. Read down and up the left page and on to the right-hand page using only your head.
8. Turn over the following page and repeat.
9. Finish reading the newspaper by bringing both hands together, then fold it or roll it up and put it underneath your arm.

Use the same technique for reading a book, but start with both hands flat together in front of you in a prayer position. Keep both hands touching each other and open your palms, like a beggar, which will show the size of the book – it's not as big as a newspaper. Read the book as you do the newspaper, and adjust your head movements to fit the size of the book.

PANTOMIME BLANCHE

'Pantomime blanche' basically means to play all characters in white-face make-up. Pantomime blanche is based on the classic Pierrot character, where the origins of white-face mime originated. The nice thing about playing Pantomime blanche is that you can play all the characters yourself.

A classic Pierrot story is where he tells the audience that he loves Columbine, but she is in love with Harlequin and it's all his (Pierrot's) fault because he is not good enough for her. He would try to kill himself by hanging but he fails even at that, and he realizes he is utterly hopeless.

Pierrot is a melancholy, hopeless romantic who never does anything right and believes everything is his fault.

A Pierrot Tale

1. Stand up straight.
2. Walk into the middle of the room by slowly lifting up your right arm so it finishes pointing at the ceiling. Slowly lift up your right leg, keeping it straight. Your left arm is out to the side, straight and horizontal.
3. Step forwards with the right leg, slowly lowering it to the ground, and bring both arms down to your sides ready to swap positions.

Pierrot starting position.

Lowering the right leg, ready to swap arm positions.

4. Now push your right heel up so you are on your toes, as you slowly lift up your straight left leg in front of you. Your left arm points up to the ceiling and your right arm points out to the right side in a horizontal position.

5. Repeat these steps until you are in the centre of your playing space. Your arms and legs need to move slowly when you walk, a bit faster than slow motion and in harmony. Pierrot is a poetic character, and if you enter quickly he becomes comic. For now, we want to avoid comedy.

6. Stop in the middle of the room. You are going to tell the audience who you are: 'I am Pierrot and I love Columbine.' With one hand point to yourself to indicate 'I'. Bring both hands together on to your chest, and then slowly down in front of you with palms facing outwards to indicate 'am'. Draw a circle around your face with a finger to indicate 'Pierrot'.

7. Make a fist with your right hand and keeping the index finger straight, move it from a low position at your side and in front of you to indicate 'and'.

Pushing back up with the right leg.

8. With your other hand point to yourself again to indicate 'I'.

9. Leaving that hand where it is, bring your other hand next to it, but place both hands on your heart to indicate 'love'.

10. Now lunge to your right side and point to invisible Columbine to indicate 'Columbine'.

11. Step back from the lunge and keep looking at Columbine.

12. This next move shows that you are going to play another character. Jump to the side and tell the audience that you are playing Columbine: 'I am Columbine and I love money!'

13. To do this repeat Pierrot's action above. For the name 'Columbine', use both hands to mime her long, wavy hair, making gestures at either side of your head, then curve your hands around the chest area to show her bust, and finish at your hips with your hands splayed out to show her dress, all to indicate 'Columbine'.

14. Use the Pierrot actions to say 'and – I – love'. As Columbine loves money, you slap both sides of your waist at the same time as if you were slapping your pockets. Then rub your thumb and fingers together to show 'money'.

15. Now jump back to the space where you were Pierrot, lunge away from Columbine, and cry. Put your hands next to your face to show the line of tears falling from your eyes. Wiggle your fingers to show the individual tears flowing. Then shrug your shoulders three times.

16. Push back from the lunge and stand up straight to notice Harlequin to your left.

17. Jump to your left so you can now play the Harlequin character.

18. Perform the same sequence as Pierrot and Columbine to mean 'I – am – Harlequin'. For 'Harlequin', use both hands to shape a moustache using the pin grip (thumb and index fingers together), pulling at the moustache on either side. Then lift both arms above your head with your fists closed to show the audience your muscles, to indicate 'Harlequin'.

19. Do the same gestures for the words 'and – I'.

20. Now slap your pockets around your waist with both hands to say 'have'.

21. Then rub your thumb and fingers together to show the word 'money'.

22. Now you can jump back to the right again to play Pierrot's reaction. You can jump to both sides and back to the centre again at any time to show when you are playing other characters.

Pierrot has his own quality of movement different to other *commedia del arte* characters. His motion is refined, precise and airy, which helps create his poetic style. He is a beautiful but tragic figure.

MIMING OBJECTS OF DIFFERENT SIZES

There are some basic principles that are useful to know so you can mime objects of different size. Practising them will help the audience see what kind of object you have in your hand so they don't misunderstand what you are doing. A rope, a pin, a newspaper, a mug and a cup of tea are all different sizes and weights, so bear these things in mind when you use mime objects.

A rope (circle grip): A rope or a pole can be shown by touching your thumb and index finger together to make a circle. Bring your other fingers close together to complete the shape.

A pin (OK grip): To pick up a small object such as a pin, a thread or a sheet of newspaper, touch your thumb and index finger together and leave the rest of the fingers apart and away from your thumb and index finger.

Circle grip.

OK grip.

A mug (semi-circle grip): Cup your hand into a semi-circle, as if you are holding a real mug, with your thumb curved round on one side and the other fingers curved round on the other side.

A ball (shell grip): When holding an object like a tennis ball or a sea shell, your fingers need to be curved and spread out, to make the shape to surround the object.

A wall (gecko hand): With a wall, a table or any other flat surface, your hands need to be flat and your fingers spread slightly apart, like the feet of a gecko.

Shell grip.

Semi-circle grip.

Gecko hand.

8
TEACHING MIME

Learning mime is about educating the body to perform physical tasks that the brain isn't familiar with. So teaching it means you have to work with how a body and brain learn new things. Repetition, breaking movements down, finding ways to explain things metaphorically, or practising with real objects, are all ways to encourage the brain to pick up new things. On a different slant, there is a fascinating read *Smart Moves Why Learning is not all in your Head* (by Carla Hannaford, PhD), which indicates that learning can be enhanced by learning with the body rather than the brain alone. Once we activate muscle memory, things become much easier to do and to re-do.

As with all teaching, all you need to do is keep things simple with an easy-to-follow and logical lesson plan. Of course it all depends how old the students are and the reason they are learning mime, but the following exercises are some of my favourite and most successful. They will be suitable for different age groups and are very basic, but are really important to know in order to start understanding mime. I believe the best way to teach is by making things fun.

THE ABC GAME

Aim: To teach key frames – one thing at a time story-telling – and the importance of posture and gesture.

1. Tell your group to stand in one big circle.
2. Explain that you will give them a letter from the alphabet, and they have to form that letter as a whole group.

3. As an example, if you give them the letter 'O', they have already made the 'O' shape as they are standing in a circle. They can make the letter standing up or lying down. It can be a capital or a lower-case letter as long as you, the teacher, can clearly identify it. The only other rule is that they have to form the letter in five seconds and before you say the word 'freeze'.
4. Then start with a simple letter 'I' for 'ink', then call 'Go! 5...4...3...2...1...freeze.'

   They should do this letter easily and most likely standing up. They may have been shouting at each other to get in line but I let that go for now!
5. Start to increase the difficulty: for example give the letter 'B' for 'balloon', 'N' for 'November' and 'Z' for 'zebra'.

   With the letters 'N' and 'Z', the group doesn't actually have to move because they are virtually the same shape, but it is interesting to see if they can work it out for themselves. If they find this easy, start asking them to create simple three-letter words such as 'cat'. They have to break up into three groups to do this, and it can start to become rather a mess, with shouting and accusations, especially when there is a five-second countdown. It doesn't matter too much if they get the word or not – what is important is that they freeze and don't speak when it gets to number one. Help them to understand that freeze *means* freeze: no one must move a muscle, or talk, or make any sound whatsoever.
6. At this point tell them they have to make a new word, but no one can talk at all. They must watch to see what has been started, and then add to the shape.

7. So, tell them they have to spell 'dog', and begin the countdown again. Go slowly with this countdown, because when the group stops talking they get the task done better and faster.

It is helpful to point this out to them now, and to ask them why they think it worked better when they weren't talking. I believe it is because they stop thinking and start acting on what's in front of them – and when under pressure, that is really all they can do. There will always be students who stop moving and stare at what the others are doing, so whilst counting down, encourage them to add themselves quickly to the shape and stop standing around.

Other Progressions of the ABC Game

1. Once you have done letters you can move on to numbers, for example '348' or '569'. It doesn't matter what it is as long as there are only three numbers – four is too many.
2. After the numbers, ask to see a 'picture' such as a photograph. An example would be the beginning of a running race.
3. Count down from five and tell them to freeze.
4. Without comment, tell them you want to see the middle part of the running race, and count down from five to freeze.
5. Finally, ask to see the last picture of a running race.

At the end of each freeze ask them to hold their positions so you can take a mime photo. Of course, you can take a real picture, too – it can be helpful for the students to see what they have done.

After this part of the exercise, you can discuss that mime is about creating shapes with the body. Shapes can make a story. The beginning, middle and end of the running race are called 'key frames', and key frames are the most important part of story-telling because they are the key moments in the story that the audience needs to see so they understand what the story is all about.

KEY FRAMES

1. Divide the group into four smaller groups. They are now going to create their own three key frames (the beginning, middle and end) of a story. These will be freeze frames, as they did with the running race. Give them a theme, such as 'the game'. They can choose any game they want, but not another running race. They have five minutes to figure out their three frames. Let them know how long they have left to complete the exercise, so there is a sense of urgency for them – it helps to put the students into action rather than to spend time on discussion.
2. At the end of the five minutes, tell them there is one rule in performing the frames that you want the audience and the actors to remember. The group that is about to perform on stage must stand in a line in the 'ready' position. You will tell the audience that they must close their eyes, which will be the cue for the performing group to move quickly and silently into their first key frame. When you say 'Open', the audience can open their eyes. Give the audience a few moments to take in the first scene, then ask them to close their eyes again while the group gets into their second position, and so on. After the third and final image when the audience has their eyes closed, the actors must return to their 'ready' position in a line. The audience can then guess what game the group were demonstrating.

It's a great experience for the audience, although as the teacher you have to watch the whole time to facilitate the process. After this exercise, talk about what worked and what didn't. Why were some games easier to guess, and some were hard? What could be done to improve the freeze frames? Here we start to get into the realm of how to use posture in story-telling, and how we can tell the audience who the characters are: their status, age, emotional state and whereabouts they are.

Re-do the exercise with all the improvements that the audience gave each group. If you have time, you could add the movement in between the key frames. For example, if it was the running race, they start in a freeze and move in slow motion to the next freeze, hold that position for a moment, and move in slow motion to the final freeze. By now the students are up and running (!), and will be aware of their body shapes; what they now have to do is hit the mark to get into their freeze position. If they had been asked to perform a mime piece without any freezes, a lot of strong postures and gestures would get lost.

THE CHARADES GAME

Aim: To teach fixed points and reference points.

A useful way to start a brand new class is by playing the game of 'charades'. This is a very well known game in which someone has to think of either a film, a television show, a song, a book or a stage show. Then they have to mime to the group what the title of it is. For example, someone chooses to mime a film title – let's say *Lord of the Rings*. So the person mimes the 'film' action (clarify the actions with the group before you start), then holds up four fingers so we know there are four words in the title of this film. To start miming the fourth word, they hold up four fingers. The mime for this fourth word might be that they point to their ring finger. A lot of people would immediately guess the full title knowing that this is the fourth word.

Make sure that everyone has a go, and pick up on their mime technique from the very beginning. When someone does the gesture for 'film', tell them to do it slowly and to stop at the end of the action. So now you have already started to teach fixed points. Every action must come to an end or a full stop before they start the next action. You

could say 'stop' or 'freeze' when each new person starts their charade. A lot of the time, students will rush through their actions and they will be unfocused and messy, so freezing is a good discipline for them to learn from the very beginning.

You could ask the group why everyone is able to guess the titles so quickly. Is everyone brilliant at mime? No. It's because everyone has a very strong reference to this game. We know what the category is and how many words there are in the title, so it is easy with this information to fill in the gaps. 'Superman' is a really easy charade because all you have to do is make the classic Superman pose. Superman has a universally recognizable physical image. Playing this game is fun and is a perfect way to get people comfortable with being physical with the group.

Once everyone has had a go, get everyone to stand in a circle and think of an object that they can mime individually for the rest of the group to guess. An example would be peeling a banana. If you peel something in the air and then take a bite it's a very easy thing to guess. I usually demonstrate this for the group and ask them why they could guess so quickly. The usual response is that there isn't anything else that you would eat in the same way. To show that you are eating a banana and not a carrot, you make a peeling action. It's a very quick reference for an observer. Remind them that whatever object they decide to mime, they must give us a strong reference to that object.

The aim of this exercise is to see how fast the audience can guess what the person is miming, so the stronger the reference, the better. If the group isn't able to guess an action and object quickly, stop and ask everyone why it is so hard to guess. The reason is usually because the group doesn't have a strong reference point. Sometimes an object needs more than one reference point to help us understand what it is.

For example, if someone is doing the mime of drinking a cup of tea and all we see them do is drink from a cup, we certainly won't know that it is supposed to be a cup of *tea*. Even if we see them make the tea, then hold a cup up and drink it, how do we know that it's not a coffee mug? Some good reference points to add would be: dipping a teabag in and out of the cup, showing us that there is a saucer (tea rather than coffee is most commonly associated with a saucer), and delicately holding the handle with your thumb and index finger (evoking the image of well-to-do ladies in a tea shop). These are strong and unique reference points to tea, and will quickly help the audience understand. Discuss as a group what reference points could be added to help other people's mimes easier to understand.

Once everyone has mimed an object or action, ask them to tell a short, two-minute mimed story about what they did before they came to class. It could be that you wake up realizing you are late, and you quickly shower and leave the house. Or it could be that you were trying to get on a train at peak hour and you had to catch the bus instead. What you are looking for is a story, so pay attention to where the person gets to in their story before it becomes too confusing and we don't know what they are doing.

After each little performance, ask the audience what was the story all about – also ask 'Was anyone confused at any point?' and 'How could we improve the mime to make it clearer?' They can then work in pairs or small groups to make up a scene entitled 'The Surprise'. By this stage, the groups are usually performing cleaner and clearer stories because they have begun to understand reference points.

SLY FOX OR GRANDMOTHER'S FOOTSTEPS

Aim: To learn tension and fixed points.

'Grandmother's footsteps' is a classic playground game and all ages love it. To recap: one person stands at one end of the room and the rest of the group stand at the other. The solo person turns their back on the group, who must try to touch that person's shoulder: the solo person turns around intermittently, and if they see anyone behind them

moving, they name that person, who must start back at the wall. The people behind them will be in a race to touch that person's shoulder first. The game ends when someone touches the person, which counts as 'catching' them. It's a very well known game so you shouldn't have a problem with people knowing how to play it.

The beauty of this game is that when the group is sneaking up, everyone is playing to win and not be seen moving. Being alive and alert is a key factor in any performance. The game becomes riveting to watch. Everyone is at a level of tension that shows a high level of urgency. This is theatre at its best! When everyone freezes, there is a magical sense of stillness (fixed point) that retains the tension and resonance emanating from everyone in the room. Adding three chairs as obstacles so people must climb over them is a great addition to the game.

Play the game three times. On the third go, take out the person who tries to catch out anyone moving. The group have to decide as a unit when the person turns around to spot them; they can send themselves back to the beginning until there is a winner. It can turn the game into a performance.

When people play the third time without the person to call them out, they may not maintain the fun and joy they had at the beginning, so remind them to remember what it was like when there was someone actually there. Perhaps step in and be the solo person for a couple of turns and step out again to help the group keep playing as if it were real.

This is a great lesson for any theatre performance, and a nice way to teach people about stage presence. Stage presence means you are always present, alive and engaged in every moment.

A SLOW-MOTION RUNNING RACE

Aim: To teach the skill of slow motion and balance.

This is a great exercise to introduce students to slow motion. Everyone starts at one end of the room and has to move in slow motion to get to the other side. The winner is the person who comes last. It's hard to cheat at this one! Before they run across the finish line everyone has to make every action and facial expression as big as possible. Play some fast paced music to juxtapose their slow motion. The aim is to see how slowly everyone can go. If they are all moving ridiculously slowly, tell them they only have five minutes left to get to the finish line and everyone must cross it. Monitor them and call out how many minutes there are left.

At the end of the race, ask what it felt like to move so slowly. A lot of people say it is hard work, and it is! What you are looking for is to see if they are aware of their whole body when it's all moving together so slowly. A lot of them will have problems transferring their weight from one leg to another. Tell them to do the exercise again using big, forward lunges and to keep their feet close to the ground. Slow motion movement requires good balance.

In a third attempt at the exercise, tell the group they have to fall in slow motion along the way. They will have to have at least two points of contact with the ground at all times. When they fall to the ground, they can use something like a push-up to control their slow descent to the floor.

After this exercise you can move on to slow-motion fighting, and I mean *ultra* slow-motion fighting. With ultra slow-motion fighting you can make actual contact without causing injury. Having done this, break them into small groups where they have to come up with a simple scene similar to slow-motion running. They have to include some very brief moments of normal time movement, which snaps back to slow motion again. So, 80 per cent slow motion with 20 per cent real-time motion. This exercise helps them learn how to control balance when moving between different speeds of motion.

You could spend all day perfecting this one exercise. Try playing epic film music as the group performs their pieces so it adds a soundscape to their performance.

POETRY

Aim: To physicalize words with the body.

This is a great exercise to express poetry physically, and can be a unique approach to learning and performing text, too. It can be done with a real poem or an improvised one, which is what I like to do first. This is done in small groups of five or six. Each group has a one-word theme, such as 'love', 'anger', 'hate' or 'fear' – anything that can stir up powerful emotions. Use one group as an example to demonstrate this exercise. The members of the group line up and face the audience. Ask the first person in the line 'what is the first word that comes into your head when I say the word "love"?' Pressure them so they don't think about it for too long – if they do, then count down from five to zero. They may say 'hurt'. Do the same for the rest of the group. The words might be 'hurt', 'joy', 'bliss', 'betrayal' or 'fun'.

Then go back to the first person and ask them to create a physical shape with their bodies for 'hurt'. If they take too long, count down again from five to zero. It doesn't matter what they do, as long as they do something physical – thinking about it defeats the purpose. Ask the rest of the group to add to the shape that they see. When I say add, I mean to extend the image further by physically connecting to the person. If someone has rolled into a ball on the ground, the other group members should echo this and make contact with it, so they are 'complicit' with the shape.

If someone does something completely different, such as standing up and pointing to the person on the ground, that means they are in conflict to the shape. It also makes the image psychological, because someone is making a comment about the person on the ground. You want to see abstract shapes echoing the original idea.

Ask them to try another shape until you see the group do something that resembles being curled up in a ball, or something that gives the essence of being hidden away. Ask them to freeze and to remember this position for the word 'hurt'. Move on to the next word, 'joy', and ask the person who found the association to start a new physical shape for 'joy'. I'm always hard on them if I think they are staying safe and just become the shape of a person who is joyful. I want to get a feeling of the word 'joy' from an abstract shape, which is far more wonderful and interesting.

Repeat the process for every word, so the group has constructed five abstract shapes for each word. They must now put them into a sentence or two that is about 'love' – their theme. As an example, it might read like this: 'Love can HURT even when there is JOY. It's the BETRAYAL of BLISS that kills off all the FUN.'

Once they have worked out the sentence for their theme, they perform it to the rest of the group. They speak the lines, one person at a time, so everyone has spoken part of the sentence. At the same time, they move into the group shape for each of their words. Once they have done that, they say the line standing up straight, not moving or acting. (This is another way to learn lines, because you create a physical connection to what you are saying.)

This is quite a wonderful thing to watch. There may be a lot of resistance from some age groups, because it's just not cool to do something so abstract, and some people are scared they will look silly. Sometimes people kick and scream and say 'I don't understand what you mean'. It's a way of stalling and trying to get out of doing the task. This does depend on where you do this, but an extraordinary number of people are not comfortable letting their bodies take the rein, and an exercise like this can be a block for some. I always tell them to stop thinking and stop talking, and just to do something.

Once the whole group is ready, do the exercise again without the words, and play some music that suits their theme.

To extend this exercise, give them real poetry. Tell the class that now they know how to bring poetry physically alive, you want to see what they do with it. They will have to learn the lines and create the shapes for some of the words. The purpose of this exercise is to demonstrate that anything can be expressed physically through mime. Shakespeare's sonnets or plays are great things to work with. If the class has to learn lines for a text-based play, you can use this exercise to help everyone learn their lines by physicalizing key words.

THE SWORD

Aim: To teach story-telling and strong postures, and to do one movement at a time.

To recap on this exercise, *see* the section 'Using Body Isolation in the Sword Exercise' in Chapter 2. It is a good follow-up to the ABC Game. Do the exercise as a mime routine first with you leading the group until they are familiar with all the steps, then divide the class into two groups. The first group will perform the routine in unison, and the other half will observe. Then the other group can perform. Ask both groups what it was like to watch individuals defending a castle: was the story simple and clear to understand? Were the movements clear and easy to read?

Once the group is reasonably familiar with the sequence, simply call out the positions very slowly from one to ten. You can speed up as you go through more repetitions. Add some variation between the speed of the steps you call out – for example, say numbers one to three quickly, followed by four to seven quickly, then eight to ten at a moderate pace. I always pause on step seven, as the group is likely to rush on to step eight before I have called it! If they do this, go back to step seven and finish the steps. Repeat the exercise in the same way, and pause again on step seven to see who remains in the moment and who will jump ahead. The idea is to train them to be present, and only to move once they hear the number called.

After calling the numbers out, go on to clap ten times, once for each step. Start very slowly, then get faster. After two of these repetitions, pause with your clap between steps seven and eight again. Ask for feedback from the group: how did it feel for them to do it this way? When clapping, the students can get lost very quickly, especially when you clap faster and faster. Explain that the reason they get lost is because they have learned the moves using numbers and not logic. When you learn your lines, do you learn them by rote, or by visualizing the progression of the story and your character? This exercise can be made a lot easier to learn by thinking about the story of the positions.

Step 1: I see a sword.
Step 2: I lunge towards the sword because I want to have a closer look.
Step 3: I like this sword so I reach for it.
Step 4: I'm near to it now, so I will take it.

And so on.

Go through all the moves with the students once again, teaching the logic/story of each movement, and how it relates to the step. Once everyone has grasped it, all the positions seem to fall into place for individuals. Go back to clapping out the exercise again, starting slowly and then getting faster. Then begin to clap faster until you reach a speed that is very fast, but not so fast that the moves can't be done with precision. Every now and then, stop at step seven. By this time the group will have greatly improved, so point out how much faster they are moving, since we eliminated calling out the numbers that equalled the positions. Ask for feedback: 'what was that like for you this time round?' I often repeat this exercise in a different lesson. It provides a strong grounding in body isolation and story-telling, and in getting students to be physically present in the room.

To develop this exercise, individuals can make up their own ten movements: for example, they have a drink at a bar, but then see another drink, so they reach for that one. As the most interesting part in the story is the decision-making section, tell them that you want to see how they deal with that moment. Instead of getting rid of the old drink, they could keep it, taste the new drink, then go back to the old drink and take a sip of that one.

You want them to make a choice between which drink to keep and which one to throw away. They can spend as long as they want in this decision-making process. There is a tendency to over-act when making the choice, so remind them that it's not about looking interesting on stage, but to be *interested in what you are doing* so your audience will be interested, too.

If you have plenty of time, take this exercise even further by getting the students to add ten extra movements before and after this section, so in total there are thirty moves, which equate to a beginning, middle and end. This is a great way towards helping students create a solo mime performance. The exercise also forces them to be precise, concise and clean with their movements within the given limitations. In the section where they have two things in their hands, there are no limits to how many moves they can make. If they take too long to decide and it gets boring, their audience will tell them in the feedback!

FIGURATION

Aim: To teach students to become inanimate objects, and to be able to transform from one shape to another.

Figuration means to create a shape, to assume a physical form that gives an impression of something. It is very useful for group story-telling. As an example: the story is about a haunted house. Someone gets lost in the woods and comes across the house. Some of the students can become the trees in the forest. It is interesting to give the forest a personality – thus the trees can swirl around with their branches reaching towards the person as they get close to the haunted house.

Start this exercise using a volunteer from the class, and tell them that you are going to be a grumpy door. Stand up straight with one arm bent and the fist clenched. Ask the volunteer to open the door, using your fist as the handle. Slowly pivot on the spot humming in a deep tone with a frown on your face, using sound to add to the mime. (Ultimately if you wanted this mime to be performed without sound, you would use live or pre-recorded sound effects; for the purposes of this exercise, you want the students to make appropriate sounds with their mime.)

Break up the class into two groups and ask them to make up a story about a haunted house. One person is the character walking in the forest, and the rest of the group play the eerie things in the setting. This will be all they need to know to create some wonderful imagery. Several people can create one object: a sofa, the grand door to the house, a table and so on. What is important is to add a personality to each object, and to make sounds with their voices. In the scene you want to see the character explore the house upstairs and downstairs, so the group has to find a way to transform from one object to another. What I mean by 'transforming' is that they have to look as if they are melting from one position to the other. You don't want to see people walking around on stage to get into another position. They can twirl or spin around and break away from one object, or transform in a way that suits the texture or personality of the object.

Give the groups a long while to practise, as it will take time to get right. You could play some appropriately creepy music to add to the performance when each group takes a turn to show their scene. At the end of their performance, always ask for feedback from the audience. Start the feedback session by asking the audience what they liked about it – this way the students/audience don't start with any negatives. Then ask where it could be improved, and finally if there was anything that wasn't understood, and if so, how it could it be made clearer.

To take figuration further, divide the class into four groups: each group must now perform a well known film in five minutes – for example *Star Wars*, *Jurassic Park*, *Batman*, *Titanic*, and so on. If the film is an epic one it will be easier for the students to create classic shapes and imagery. They can use sound effects and sound bytes (one-liners), but must keep the text to a minimum of three sentences. Again you want to see how quickly and cleverly they can transform from shape to shape. They need to focus on the key moments in the film that most of the audience will know, otherwise they will lose their interest very quickly. The groups show their piece to each other, and a feedback session can follow in the same vein as before.

If you wanted to take the exercise further, you can use text from a play; the people who don't have any lines to speak can become the set and personality of the scene. Instead of the speaking characters leaving the stage when they finish, they can become part of the set and can wait for their next entrance from there. This is a wonderful way to give everyone a role, and to keep everyone on stage, too.

THE SEVEN LEVELS OF TENSION

Aim: To teach different levels of physical tension in performance.

This can be a great exercise for students to learn how physical tension in the body can tell a story. If the students are younger, exchange the nightclub setting for an art gallery. They are so bored in the gallery that they have fallen asleep so they are set up to start at level one.

Having done the basic version of the exercise, get seven volunteers on stage and give them a number each from one to seven. Number one is going to be the lowest status, and seven the highest. The setting is a smart restaurant. Talk them through the whole exercise. The exercise is now about the level of status that can be portrayed through tension.

Level 1: Number one starts the scene by lying down, with the rest of the volunteers off at stage right. Number one is a trainee cleaner in the restaurant; it's very early in the morning, and they have fallen asleep on the job. Every now and then they can check their watch sheepishly and go back to sleep. Call on number two to enter.

Level 2: Number two is also a cleaner, but he is number one's boss. Number two walks in very slowly and nudges number one to get off the floor. Number one slowly gets up and equals the same level of tension as number two, and they both walk very sluggishly around the room as they clean up the kitchen. Call in number three.

Level 3: Number three is the boss of the cleaning company, and comes in to inspect the two cleaners who have been hired. He is very economical and efficient, and points out to them where they have missed a spot on the floor or on a pan. The other two pick up on his level of tension and move around in the same way, becoming more efficient in their cleaning. Call in number four.

Level 4: Number four is the sous chef, who sees that the cleaning job is very average and not up to standard. Moving around casually, he makes the cleaners and the boss pick up their pace to do a better job. Once again, all characters pick up the same rhythm and tension as the new character who has just walked in. Call in number five.

Level 5: Number five is the head chef, who enters rather excited because a brand new menu has been made for the restaurant. The head chef hurries everyone up to get the kitchen ready. All characters below him now move to his pace and level of energy, and start to hurry around the kitchen. Now call in number six.

Level 6: Number six is the owner of the restaurant. The owner runs on stage and tells everyone that the health inspector has just arrived and the kitchen has to be immaculate. There is chaos, and everyone runs around tidying whilst the owner gives orders. Call in number seven.

Level 7: Number seven is the health inspector, who quickly enters the stage and stops abruptly. Everyone else runs to stand in line, as if a drill sergeant had entered the room: they all stand to attention petrified. The health inspector is very intense, and slowly walks around the room checking for dust on the cooking stove, pots and pans. Tell number seven that everything is up to standard, and he can nod and leave the room.

You can then play the story in reverse order: as soon as the inspector leaves, the owner (number six) hurries everyone around the room to double check everything is clean, and everyone below him does the same. He tells everyone he is going out of the room to make sure the health inspector has actually left the building, and exits. The head chef (number five) takes over, and slows down his pace because of his excitement about the new menu. He tells everyone he is off to write it all down, and exits the stage. The sous chef (number four) takes charge, and everyone is now working at his casual, everyday pace. The sous chef tells them all that he is going to buy some food, and exits. The boss of the cleaners (number three) now takes charge, and goes back to his own level of economy, and the other two follow suit. Telling his employees that they are doing a great job, the boss cleaner exits. The cleaner (number two) now takes over, and orders the trainee cleaner around apathetically, and the trainee cleaner mimics his tension and energy level. The cleaner says his job is done, and leaves. The trainee cleaner (number one) is now exhausted after the whole episode, and collapses to the floor and falls asleep.

After this demonstration, divide the class up into groups of seven. If there are odd numbers, people can double up in the same role – for example, there can be two trainee cleaners, two owners, or two inspectors. The groups have to come up with a situation where they can play all the levels, and it scales up and back down again. I remember seeing a group do a very funny version of fitness fanatics in a gym: the person playing number seven played a famous person and she did hardly anything, whilst everyone else watched her in absolute awe.

9
CREATING A MIME PERFORMANCE

Hopefully you have been inspired and tried out some of the mime techniques, tips and tricks from the previous chapters. This chapter looks at different things to think about to create a mime performance, but there should be some useful things that can be applied to other types of show as well.

KNOW YOUR AUDIENCE

The audience is king: without them there is no show, and whatever you do, your job is to entertain them. Connect to them and get them on your side. But before you can do this, the first thing you need to know is, who are your audience? If your show isn't tailored to the right audience, it won't matter how good it is, it simply won't work to its full potential.

I once took a mime show up to the Edinburgh Fringe Festival thinking that it would blow everyone away. However, it was performed on the street with the audience walking by, the street was very noisy, and there was a lot of competition from other artists. The show was about a handyman getting lost in a wonderful, fantastical mime world, and it died a quick death because the audience was a street audience, moving past quickly with a noisy and busy background. I realized I needed to do something very quick and dramatic, or big and bold, something that grabbed their attention, backed up with a very loud sound system.

Over the course of the next two weeks I worked on it every night to bring it up to speed, but no matter what I did to save my show, it didn't work.

In the end it had to be rewritten so that it had a loose storyline rather than a detailed one. Think visual cabaret show and you get the idea. The idea of my show was a good one, and it works really well for a theatre audience, but as the saying goes: 'No such thing as a bad audience, only a bad show.'

Know your audience well if you want half a chance to produce a good show. If you don't know who they are, do the research first. What are the age ranges? Young? Teenage? Primary school children? Middle age? Elderly? Foreign? What is the setting for your show? A cabaret? Theatre? On the street? An arts festival? Art installation? Talent show? Cruise ship? If you are performing to a street crowd, an outdoor arts festival or a cabaret audience, the show will have to be visually dynamic and simple. There is no time for a detailed storyline. You have to perform your number one hits at a dynamic pace, or do one simple thing really well. Examples of this may be a 'following show', in which you mimic passersby, or you can do slow-motion walking, or perform as a living statue. This applies to most outside audiences, or in a setting where the general public just happens to be there. The exception is in the theatre, when people have specifically come to see you.

With a cabaret show your audience is likely to be inside a venue, but they have come to eat and drink and to be entertained at the same time. You are just a part of the experience, and not the sole reason they are there. So the above rules apply for this type of audience as well. For an artistic installation you can just about get away with doing anything you

Halloween street festival, mime act.

want, as it is 'art'. Your audience may not connect to what you are doing, and may ask what it's all about, but you can always get away with the line: 'It's whatever you want it to be!' However, this can come over as arrogant and disconnecting. You want to make sure the audience has been entertained, challenged and moved by what they have experienced.

If you are performing in a talent show, you need to think more of a cabaret audience, and create something that is dynamic and simple. A slow-moving, living statue will become very boring, very quickly, unless you can think of a way to surprise the audience, whereas in a theatre you can take time to explore a detailed story because your audience is there for you.

Ultimately, whatever your story is in mime, you must always keep it simple and easy to follow – you can fill in details later. Theatre is a wonderful space to perform in, as you have a captive audience with no outside distractions and you are in control of the environment you are going to be performing in. You can use lighting, sound and

video effects, and set design, and you can take more time on stage, and come to points of complete stillness in the theatre.

WHAT KIND OF SHOW DO YOU WANT TO DO?

What kind of show do you want to create? Comedy? Drama? Political? Tragedy? Farcical? A sketch show? A parody? Satirical? Historical? A mixture of any or all of these? It is usually best to do the show that *you* would want to see: it's your kind of theatre if it's what *you* want to see, and it's unlikely to be like other shows around. Imagine that you are going to create the very show that would excite *you* to watch – how exciting would it be to create and actually perform it?

Start visualizing what *you* would want to see, then get up and start improvising around your vision. You can start with something simple, such as 'I would like to see a mime show about...'. Don't make any judgements about whether it's a good idea or not – there is no such thing, it's your first idea and a starting point. Set up a camera or your phone to record what you do, and start to improvise for a few minutes; then stop and watch it over. If you don't have an outside director or someone to give feedback, then using video will help you to see what works and what doesn't, and will prompt ideas for what you can do next time.

When we were in the stages of rehearsing a show we did this year, the most important thing for us was to do a show that we were excited about. We wanted to do a comedy, which had a good story mixed with some dramatic and epic moments. This got us excited enough to work long hours and to a deadline, because we loved our story and really hoped the audience did too!

SIMPLICITY: K.I.S.S.

K.I.S.S. stands for 'Keep It Simple, Stupid!', and this saying is the best advice I know for devising a mime show. It's not about dumbing the show down, it's about making it easy to follow and not over-complicating it. Sometimes when students are given a theme for their solo mime piece, such as 'The Game', the story can be very complicated, so that it's difficult to know what it's all about. The piece may start off in a normal setting, such as a house, but suddenly the character has entered a time loop, as in the film *Groundhog Day*: the scene repeats itself, but now the character has become a superhero!

There is nothing wrong with that, and of course it's quite possible to do, but only if there is a clear and simple logic to follow so we understand it. The best mime pieces are the simplest ones, such as eating breakfast in the morning and being late for work. An audience has a very strong reference to this in their own lives, and the journey of the character in this simple story can be riveting. I have seen a fantastic piece about someone day-dreaming that they are a superhero whilst at work. The transition from everyday life to the fantastical was so brilliantly executed, we knew that the daydream was a daydream and not a complete shift in story.

You can do everything in mime, which is one reason it is so exciting to perform and watch – just remember 'K.I.S.S.'!

DESIGNING THE MUSIC, LIGHTS, SET, PROPS, COSTUME AND MAKE-UP

Costume

So now you know what kind of show you want to do, you know your audience, and you have kept your piece nice and simple, you need to get the show ready for performance. What costume are you going to be wearing? A pair of black trousers with a black top and black shoes is a costume. The traditional French mime costume is easy to source if you go down that route. Black trousers/skirt, a black-and-white stripy top (navy or sailor shops are good for this, but they have also been

back in fashion and are easily purchased in high-street shops) and a black beret, which you can get anywhere. Black-and-white stripy socks can be found in random little shops, and footwear can be black trainers or jazz shoes (get these from dance shops). Your shoes can add to, or hinder your movement. Slippery soled shoes can be great if you perform some mime walks, but not if you are running around. On the other hand, rubber-soled shoes may be too sticky on the floor, which will impede quick movements.

You can also wear character-specific costume with stage make-up. The style of your show and your personal preferences will dictate what kind of costume you choose for your performance. If your show is clown based, you could style the costume with more colour. Perhaps you want a more artistic, fashionable look, so hunt down items that will do that for you. It can take time to source these items, but it is very exciting to find them, so keep a lookout in unlikely places for irregular bits of costume.

Try your show with your costume on prior to performance – it will be hard to pull off a good mime piece with restrictive or tight clothing and the wrong shoes. Bear in mind the surface you will be playing on because you run the risk of injuring yourself if you are moving quickly and performing falls.

Make-up

If you want to go down the traditional white-face make-up route it's easy to do. You have a choice between water- or grease-based make-up. They have different advantages. Water-based make-up is very easy to put on and take off. Its disadvantage is that if you sweat a lot, or you are performing under hot stage lights, the make-up can run, dry out or crack. Grease paint doesn't run or crack, it looks better than water-based paint, and you can dab powder over the grease to give it a smooth, professional look. Its disadvantage is that it is more expensive and takes longer to get off your face – so if you perform and then have to be somewhere else soon afterwards, the grease will make you late!

Applying face make-up.

If it gets on your costume it could stain, whereas water-based make-up will come out in the wash. Whichever one you choose, here are the steps to put on the traditional white-face make-up.

PUTTING ON WHITE-FACE MAKE-UP

You will need:

White-face paint-base make-up (either grease- or water-based)
Red lipstick/red lipliner
Black eyeliner pencil/mascara
A mirror
Pencil sharpener
White base powder
Moisturizer/face wipes/coconut oil/cotton pads

1. Moisturize your face with face cream. This will make removal of the make-up a lot easier, especially if you use the grease-based white.

2. Apply the white base to your face. You can use your fingers to do this, but some people like to use a make-up sponge. Professional make-up artists do this, but you can achieve the same effect with your fingers if you don't mind your fingers getting messy. Smooth the make-up all over your face from the top of your forehead, around the edges of your face (don't cover the ears), and finish it off around your mouth and just under your chin. White face paint is the hardest of all colours to make look really smooth, but spend some time smoothing it out so it doesn't look patchy. The effect you want to create is like a full white face mask. Use a face wipe and finish off the edges, especially around your jaw line and underneath your chin. Wipe off any excess make-up. If you are using grease paint, powder down the base by dabbing a make-up pad/puff on top of the grease. This will help keep the grease dry and firm if you get hot.

3. Apply the black eyeliner underneath your eye following the line of the lashes. You can do the top lids as well. This can be quite difficult and time-consuming, particularly for males, and isn't always necessary, but I would recommend doing both lids for a female. Use the mascara to add more definition around the eyes.

4. Use a black eyeliner pencil to darken your eyebrows so they stand out. You can follow the line of your brow, or create different shapes, which will change the expression on your face. Play around with it to see which look suits your mime character.

5. Use red lipliner to clear up the edges between the white base and the lips. Use the lipstick to fill in the rest.

6. To remove the make-up, it is helpful to use face wipes first, followed by coconut oil, using a clean face wipe to rub off the excess oil; then moisturize your face and get the base out of your wrinkles and pores. If possible, wash with soap and water.

You may want to have black lips instead of red, though red is popular as it's the only colour in a traditional French mime costume and it highlights the lips and lifts them from the face.

You may want to add a tear or two to either cheek, which pays homage to the Pierrot character. I like to keep my make-up as simple as possible so my face doesn't have a set character look.

The best place to source white grease-based make-up is in a theatrical make-up shop. The white base has to be *white*, and not the sort of pale foundation base that you can get at any average make-up shop. Lipliners, mascara, lipstick and eyeliners you can get anywhere. Base powder you can probably get at a general make-up shop too, although the theatrical ones are the best. Face wipes and coconut oil you can find in supermarkets or in health food shops.

If you are starting out, I would suggest using a water-based white, which you can easily source online. If you want to get serious and you are going to be performing often and professionally with a white face, then definitely invest in grease paint. It's expensive but will last a very long time, and you will look the business, too.

The Set

As a mime artist you create your own mime set so you don't really need a physical one. If you do use a set, it only has to be minimal; for example, you might want to use a chair or table and some stage flats to make effective exits and entrances. The beauty of mime is that you create the world around you. The less you have on stage, the more the audience will use their own imagination to see the environment that you mime for them.

Lights

When you can light your mime show you have a great opportunity to focus on particular moments in your story. If your character is feeling lonely, or sad, or is thinking of something important that you want to highlight, a spot light (also called a 'special') will work really well. Use a general wash for lighting the whole stage, and use colours to add mood and ambience to the scene.

If your show is a light comedy, your lights will be best if they are bright, otherwise the comedy won't play well and it may appear to be a dark comedy – darker lighting dampens a comic effect. If you don't have much choice with your lighting, get the lights as bright as you can so your audience can see your actions and facial expressions. Details can get lost on a dimly lit stage. Unless you are lucky, you won't get much choice about your lighting, so try and get as bright a space as possible to perform in.

I once performed a short comedy mime show at an event where the lighting technician changed the lights to blue, green and red, seemingly at will, which did not help my show's impact or my concentration! White, bright light is much less distracting.

Props

It is usually best only to use props if they are crucial to the story. Marcel Marceau performs a wonderful mime sketch called 'The Lion Tamer' in which he uses a hoop and mimes everything else, including the lion. The hoop gives the audience an excellent visual reference and is crucial to his scene. In another of his sketches, 'The Tango Dancer', he uses a wallet as a prop and mimes everything else, including the woman he is tango dancing with. The story is that the woman is trying to steal his wallet from his back pocket.

There are times when an object is really hard to mime effectively and it is vital to your story, so a prop can be very handy in this instance. Don't just use props because you can. Cull what isn't necessary to your story, and you will always create a good piece. For example, if you were doing a show about a magical hat that had its own life, then use a real hat and mime that it gets heavy and light, that it floats in one direction and then another. This is what the whole story is about, so it works. If you tried on a hat in the scene and it wasn't a big part of your story, there would be no point in using a real hat as a prop. It wouldn't be a mime show if we used real props all the time!

Music

The most important thing with music is to make sure the music you use is copyright free. If you use commercial music, check that your performance venue covers the copyright so you can use the music in your show legally. A good method is to buy copyright-free music on the internet and mix it with sound effects as you devise your piece. Music works really well with mime, as it creates a sound-scape for your show. It also lifts the performance by giving it atmosphere, and sets the tone of your show. Sound effects always highlight mime and take the show to another level.

You might want to work with a musician so you can have a live underscore in your show. A golden rule when using music and mime together is not to use music with words in, otherwise the audience will try to match the words in the song to the story in your mime, and if you are not performing with the words in mind, the mime and music will seem disjointed and out of place.

Having said all that, you can of course perform without any music or effects. Marceau used music followed by silence in his shows to create dramatic moments. Think about using silence as much as music!

ALWAYS TEST OUT THE SHOW FIRST

Many new shows have failed simply because they weren't tested out first. This year we had got to the stage of having a structure for a mime theatre show, and had blocked out the basics of the scenes. We arranged to rehearse the show in the theatre two months before performance. It was a disaster! We had been rehearsing and devising the show in a small space, knowing that the stage was much larger than our rehearsal space, but rehearsing what we had in theatre, we realized it simply wasn't going to work as we hadn't created a story big enough to fill the large stage. Luckily we had carefully scheduled developing and

rehearsing our piece, so we found this out with plenty of time to spare. Create the story you want to see, but try it in your performance space before you perform it! You should then know whether it feels right or not.

You can test out a new show by performing it in front of your target audience to get their initial reactions. You can do a question-and-answer session with them afterwards, or ask them to fill in pre-arranged feedback forms so they can leave them with you after the show. One of the best things to ask first is, what did they like about the show? Second, was there anything they didn't understand? What was confusing? These are simple enough questions that an audience can answer, and they will give you a good insight into what can be improved on, and what you can do more of.

It's best to test out your show on a neutral audience and not with friends or family, as you need honest feedback. If you can get an outside director to look at your show, that would be perfect. Testing it out in different places would be even better! Sometimes you can just test out one or two sections of it. Try a cabaret or a variety club with a new show to see how it works with that kind of an audience. If it works in a cabaret setting with all the distractions of buying and serving drinks, with half the audience talking to each other, and they still understand and enjoy it, then you know you are doing something right, and your piece is likely to work anywhere.

Alternatively you can film yourself performing the show, and then ask someone to watch it for you to see if they understand what is happening.

THE PERFORMANCE

So you've created your show, you know your audience, and you have tested it out. You are now ready to perform. Wherever you are performing, you need to prepare yourself for the show. Do a physical warm-up prior to the performance: stretch your legs, arms, neck and back, and massage

Silent movie comedy show.

your face. Warm up your voice, too, with some tongue twisters. Why? Because your voice is also a part of your body. Warming up your tongue and mouth helps to articulate your facial expressions.

Also, if you know you are going to be performing a mime show on a certain date, keep your fitness levels up for as long as you can prior to it. In an ideal world, maintaining your fitness should be a priority in your everyday life. The stronger and more flexible a mime artist is, the more range, balance and definition they can add to their mime. This should apply to any performer. The work we do is hard, with long hours, and the healthier and stronger our bodies are, the more stamina and endurance we have to be on top of our game.

WORKING WITH OTHER MIME ARTISTES

Mime Duos

Working with someone else can add great character relationships to a show, and you can build even more wonderful illusions. In a pair you can mime carrying a plank of wood or a sheet of glass – though you would really have to practise keeping the mime plank the same size when you pick it up and carry it around. Classic pair scenarios include boy meets girl, a waiter serving food to a customer in a restaurant, someone getting their

Mime theatre show.

the essence and feel of city life. The group can walk around on stage quickly, turning left or right at sharp angles in a grid formation with blank faces as if they are part of a machine. The group could walk around randomly, and to draw focus, one member of the group could walk very slowly in the random pattern. The audience will look at the person walking slowly, and it can be a great starting point for a story.

This is a simple exercise to try out, and could result in inspiring you to build an entire show. You could use this walking around exercise, perhaps to music, and start to form different paced lines in the space. Someone could stop all of a sudden, turn their head and look at everyone else walking around in their own world – what a wonderful image for the audience to dream around. See how easily you can create wonderful images and ideas using figuration or by changing the tempo and rhythm of walking *en masse*. Add in some relationships, and there is a show right there for you.

hair cut by a hairdresser, doctor and patient, criminal and policeman/woman, taxi driver and the customer, the driving instructor and learner, teacher and student – and so on. The thing to focus on as a pair is the relationship between the two characters, which is going to make the story interesting. You can perform a technically brilliant piece of mime, but unless your show has a solid story based around characters and their relationship to each other, your audience won't warm to them or the story.

KEEP PRACTISING

It does take time and effort to get good at the mime illusions and to find your own unique way of moving. The more you play and practise, the more you can discover for yourself. You can learn the steps of an illusion, but only time will make them ready to pull off in the pub or in performance. When working on a new illusion it's helpful to spend twenty minutes a day practising it with a partner or in front of a mirror to perfect the look of it. You could spend a small amount of time practising slow-motion walking, and on a different day, see what you can do to expand your range of facial expressions. Always do a stretch before you begin so your body is warmed up beforehand.

The more you practise, the more you will discover, and the more you will think up new ways of doing things. When you come up with something new, film yourself and watch it back so you can make constant improvements. When you are at

Mime Groups

If you decide that you want to work in a group of three or more, then you have a perfect opportunity to create images as a whole group ('figuration'). A nice example of group work is creating a cityscape. Make basic images that give the audience this level, working with someone who understands mime will help you even more.

I have done a lot of film, television and corporate work when a director specifically wants a mime artist, and each time I have been required to do something that I have never done before. This is very challenging, as mime is such a broad area: it covers mimicry mime, illusionary mime, technical mime, character mime, animal mime, movement vocabulary, 'following show' mime, slapstick comedy mime and hand mime. When I worked on *Avengers: Age of Ultron*, I had people holding down my right leg, as I walked like a robot. Dragging them along behind me made the movement resemble a dysfunctional robot, which wasn't suitable, so I was asked to wear a skateboard on one leg instead. Prepare yourself and your body as much as you can for any eventuality!

On another occasion I had to film a corporate video on green screen and draw a smooth, curved line in the air, and in the same shot, draw a wiggly line starting at the original point that went upwards. Anyone could have done the line drawing, but the points in the air had to be exactly precise so that in post production they could create graph lines with video graphics that matched my finger movements. Mime artists develop a lot of body and spatial awareness, so although this was challenging, it was probably somewhat easier for me than someone else who hadn't spent the time getting to know how and where their body moves in space.

My point is simple: the more you practise, the more experience you will gain, which will be vital preparation when you are under pressure and have to come up with the right performance on the spot.

SIMPLICITY

Simplicity! Simplicity! Simplicity! This has already been mentioned, but it is so important, I am mentioning it again. When you start creating a mime piece that is longer than ten minutes, you will discover something unique to this theatre form. Because you cannot reference time, place, development or situation with words, you find yourself racking your brains as to what you can do to make the audience understand. It really is worth doing this: your audience will be grateful and will enjoy your piece more because they don't have to work to make sense of it.

USE OF STEREOTYPES

Using character stereotypes is going to help make your mime easy to understand because your audience will be able to make quick associations and references. A British policeman (*aka* 'bobby') stands up straight with his chest out and his chin tilted slightly upwards; he walks with his hands behind his back, and stops and occasionally bobs up and down. He would look down over his nose, and his eyes rapidly move around to look out for troublemakers. Obviously policemen don't bob up and down anymore, but it is a stereotype that the majority of people will recognize. Once the audience recognizes the character you are playing, you can do what you want in the scene because they know who you are and what your position and status is.

You could find other ways to play a 'bobby', but if the audience doesn't know who you are, then you risk losing them. They will always be trying to work out who you are supposed to be, and no matter what action or story you perform after your character's introduction, you will have left them behind and they will quickly become uninterested, frustrated or bored. You never want this. It means the audience stops playing the 'game of pretend' with you, and they might see you as a bad performer or an amateur who doesn't care for them. This is the greatest insult, and your reputation as a mime artist will be shot down in flames. Use stereotypes as a quick way into characterization.

A basic rule for this is that the audience needs to understand within three seconds of being on

The Joker.

stage who you are, otherwise it is 'game over'. If you can make it clear who your character is without the use of stereotypes, then do it. A voiceover, sign or costume can help. The show could start with a voiceover saying: 'Jane was the best police officer in the force.' Or someone comes on stage with a sign that reads: 'The life of a police officer.' The most obvious is to wear a police costume! It doesn't really matter how you do it, but you must.

SENSE OF PLAY

I believe that all good theatre is based on play. What I mean by 'play' is joyfully playing the game of 'make believe'. There is no method acting in mime: performing mime is about imagination being brought to life in a light and joyful way, even if you are performing the story of someone

or something bad. You are creating a world from nothing, making the 'invisible, visible'. When you start to perform, the audience must see the light in your eye and the enjoyment that you have as you play the game of pretend. If your character is sad, we must see that you enjoy playing at being sad. We must see you enjoy playing the meanest ruler of the world or the depressed king of homelessness.

It doesn't matter what action or state your character is in, if you are enjoying it, your audience will love you for it because they will enjoy you having fun with what you do. They will enjoy this game you have created, and they will want to play this game with you too. Acting that is thrust upon them invades their personal space, and no one likes that. Imagine an actor on stage being genuinely angry, or truly sad, and we may feel a sense of empathy, but we don't get pleasure from feeling it. The show has then lost its lightness and sense of play. What the audience experiences is raw emotion forced upon them, and their imagination has no space to roam and dream. The show will lose its poetic ability and can push an audience away, leaving them cold and isolated.

We enjoy watching children play, because they believe in their game of cops and robbers or princesses. So be child-like in your play and let your audience have an opportunity to enjoy your performance.

THE ESSENCE OF...

Performing anything in mime is really about performing the essence of something. If you are playing a giant, you must display the physical essence of being very tall and very heavy. You can use the slow-moving earth element to help (*see* Chapter 3 The Elements). Playing someone who is nervous and anxious you may use the fire element to get to the essence of that emotional state. You need to study and learn what the very essence of something is, so that you can physicalize it very quickly and cleanly for an audience.

What is the essence of someone having a nervous breakdown? The simple answer is that they break down. A nervous breakdown has got to do with the person's mind and emotions. You could fall into a trap and demonstrate a breakdown like this, but you would be missing the point and would lose the potential poetry available in the physical expression of this. Think differently. Find a material, or an object, or something that changes its state physically from one thing to another. For example, a sugar cube dissolves in a glass of hot water. Try to replicate this transition and 'break down' as a mime artist. Slowly allow your legs to give way as the water 'erodes' you, fall to your knees, then on to all fours, and slowly your arms 'break down' until you are flat on your stomach. Repeat this several times so you get the feeling of breaking down physically.

Once you have embodied this feeling, add it to a scene: for example, you have just received a letter with some bad news in it, which devastates you. Using what you have just practised with the erosion of the sugar cube, collapse slowly to the floor. What was written in the letter is the hot water, and it is affecting the sugar cube, which is you. An audience won't know that you are using the physicality of a dissolving sugar cube, but the mechanics and physics of what is happening will mean they can relate to it on a subconscious level.

As a mime, it's not your job to feel things, it's your job to make the audience feel things for themselves, to give them the essence of… (something) so their own imaginations do all the work: this offers a deeper experience than something that can actually be seen. Think of the difference between reading a book and watching a film. Your mind sees the people and places in the book, and this can often be so much stronger and more meaningful to you than someone else's vision which has been made concrete in a film.

Ultimately your aim as a mime artist is to give people something visual that is also wonderful and beautiful, so you offer your audience something that resonates with them on a profound level. Jean Louis Barrault calls this 'poetry', while Irene Mawer recognized that mime can make anything beautiful or ugly, right or debased full of 'truth and beauty'. When you delve into any art form deep enough, you get a chance to experience the breadth of human existence and spirituality, with your artistry being the magic carpet ride to get there.

Trade show – miming cocktail waiter.

10
USING MIME IN EVERYDAY LIFE

BODY LANGUAGE

Whatever you do in life, mime applies to everything that is physical. You might need to give a presentation, or a speech at a wedding, or you might be a model walking down the catwalk, doing a voiceover for a commercial, or you need to ask your boss for a pay rise: in each situation you can't do anything without using your body. Your voice is a part of your body, and without your body you can't speak. Your body is the base of the pyramid, and the voice is the tip at the top. You can take away the tip of the pyramid but not the base.

First impressions create a big impact. As soon as you enter a room, your body is giving away a wealth of information, a language that most people can subconsciously hear. We can sense if someone has low self-esteem, is nervous, arrogant, insincere, closed or egotistical. Everyone wants to be loved, but our insecurities sometimes get in the way and we become defensive and it gets hard to be our true selves. The body doesn't lie, and no matter how we try to hide, protect or project otherwise, your body's posture and gestures will leave an impression with people. There are some very simple things you can do to create a great impression wherever you are and with whatever you have to do. Quite simply, all you have to do is connect to your body.

Pull Upwards

As a general rule, the best way to create a good first impression is to be open and available to give and receive. If you are standing up, stand up straight and to your full height. If you are sitting down, sit up straight. If you stand or sit with a slumped posture,

it may be read (sometimes wrongly!) that you have an inverted emotional state. It might also read that you are tired, lazy, depressed, lethargic, defensive, indifferent, apologetic. Slumping the body literally means that you haven't got the energy to pull upwards and fight against gravity.

> [...] you are focused, you give energy out and you receive it. You communicate spontaneously and listen well, you are generous and people are generous in return.
>
> *from 'Presence' by Patsy Rodenberg*

People who are winners – happy, positive, fun, excited, confident – have the energy to push upwards physically. They are not afraid to show their true height and stature. They pull upwards to show their full selves and claim their physical space.

Furthermore, if you have adopted a slumped posture, over a period of time it will take effort to retrain and strengthen the muscles so it is conformable for you to sit and stand with a healthy curved spine (look this up online). And how much are you affecting your organs if you are constantly hunched over? Your posture doesn't just affect how you can be perceived, but it affects your physical health as well.

Open Your Body

People who are defensive and protective physically close off their body. Their chest is either slumped in, or pushed out forcefully to over-compensate. The chest needs to be open and relaxed, which will help naturally drop and pull back the shoulders, immediately giving you a more erect posture. The chest is a very vulnerable area because it is close to our emotional centre and our heart, the very thing that keeps us alive. Once you open this vulnerable area to people, they will want to connect to you. People connect to those who are open and vulnerable, because you become approachable and lovable. Forceful people who project themselves on to others, who crush your hand in a handshake, talk over you and hide things (even if they think they are doing it for a good reason) are not really open to listening to you.

Being open means that you can give of yourself in a conversation both verbally and physically, which also makes you available to listen to and receive the other person. An open body simply means facing another person straight on, pulling your body upwards, with your chest open and shoulders back, and genuinely listening to whoever is talking to you.

EYE CONTACT

Listening to someone means that you have eye contact with them. When you listen to someone with a sincere smile behind your eyes you will make contact with them on a deeper level. If the eyes wander, then it is a sign that you are thinking of something else while they are talking, perhaps getting ready for them to pause so you can start talking! For them, it will feel that you are not giving them the time to finish what they are saying. If you wait for them to finish what they are saying and maintain eye contact, they will be more open to listen to your response. Maintaining eye contact means that you are paying attention, and people will feel that they have been seen, and will feel appreciated and respected.

BE TRUTHFUL

Being truthful about yourself is about declaring yourself in the moment. If you are about to give a speech in front of a lot of people and you are nervous, tell your audience that you are nervous! They have probably already picked up on this, and once you declare the truth, they will love you for it, because you become real and genuine to them in that moment. Don't be apologetic about being nervous – this is like asking for sympathy, and can create an awkward feeling for them. Be open and truthful. Say it as a matter of fact. It will show everyone that you have the confidence to be truthful about yourself in front of others, and displays strength and confidence about yourself. People hate things that are fake, and love the truth. It can be hard to be open and honest, sometimes more so with people you are close to, but you can let anyone see your vulnerability: ironically, it's one thing that makes you stronger in the eyes of everyone else.

THINK EVERYTHING IS WONDERFUL

When we think everything is wonderful, it affects us physically, too. Try walking around the room, standing up straight and making yourself believe that everything is wonderful and amazing. You will find it really hard to be sad, down or depressed. We are what we think: it affects us physically, and vice versa. Try walking very slowly around the room, dragging your feet, slumping your shoulders and looking at the ground, at the same time trying to think you are strong, confident, and that everything is wonderful. It's a very hard thing to do. Even if you can manage it, your energy won't be centred in your body. It's like trying to run up a hill with lead weights tied around your ankles.

Now try it again, but this time walk around the room standing up straight, head held high, walking with confidence, chest open and thinking wonderful thoughts. Be open to give and receive in the moment. Physically and mentally, you are now in harmony with yourself on all levels. This is what we call in the theatre 'stage presence' because you are now present in the moment, in the here and now.

It doesn't matter what you are doing or where you are, you can connect to this energy at any time.

PHYSICAL EXERCISE

Physical exercise sharpens the mind, and gives you physical and mental confidence as well. People in warm and hot countries are all very physically expressive. The Italians talk with the hands, the Australians are very open and direct and have a strong sporting and outdoor culture, the South Americans have a strong connection to dance and music. Daily physical activity will awaken your body and enliven your mind. You become more aware of your movements and your body's range of motion and strength, and you will begin to learn about yourself. The more you learn, the more confidence you will have.

Doing physical activity twenty to thirty minutes a day, six days a week will dramatically improve your health and physical confidence. You can do anything that means you move your body a bit differently for a while: stretches, weight training, walking the dog, yoga – literally anything that means you move and change your heart rate. Eat well, sleep well, and don't forego life's pleasures even when you are working at full capacity. Your life will dramatically improve, as you will find a new source of energy that will make it easy for you to pull upwards and onwards.

For working actors and performers, there is a big difference between being able to play a role as you are, and performing the role from a place of fitness and health. How well are you going to succeed when you are under pressure and having to come up with things that test you physically and mentally if your body is ill prepared? And if you do find yourself coping without having to look after yourself, enjoy it, but start thinking about your health as you get older – your body might not thank you for having to endure so much at a young age.

GET OFFLINE AND GET IN LINE

We live in a very visual and digital age where online media is constantly swamping us with a relentless stream of images and information. In today's smartphone society, it has become very easy to be distracted. But the more we allow these distractions to become a part of our lives, the less we become physically engaged in life. There is a time and place for emails and social media, and it needs to be limited. The body is designed to move, and your mind needs to be in line with what the body is doing. The mind needs to be free of distractions, and able to focus on what really needs to be done.

It is interesting that when we are physically engaged and the mind is free of unnecessary things, the brain seems to become more open to problem solving, creativity and clear thinking. If you want to solve a problem, if you have a creative block, or you need to find an answer to something, get up and do something that you don't have to think about. Move away from online babble, go for a walk in the park, potter in the garden, go for a train ride or have a shower. Have you ever noticed that your best ideas or problem-solving abilities get better when you are not thinking about them?

When you exercise, by all means listen to music sometimes, but also take some time to move your body in silence. Start to feel the small things inside you that you can only start hearing when you have no noise around you and you can go inwards. The more you do this, the more you will become bodily aware, which will help you in all manner of ways. You'll take a rest when you know you need one, you will know when you are slumping and remember to stand up straight again, and will notice the more subtle changes in your body as you get fitter.

The digital age has got our heads down and focused on the screens, which can make our bodies isolated, inactive and not appreciated for what they give us or for their power. Get in line with yourself – be unbalanced and know you are, be short of breath and know you are, be aware of your limitations, and appreciate all of it. We like to avoid connecting to our bodies – we have an epidemic of body-conscious, unhealthy and unhappy people in our society. Just accept what and where you are inside your body, and give yourself a break. This will be the first step to becoming more in contact with who you and what your body really is.

11

MIME AND BEYOND

MIME FOR STAGE AND SCREEN

I originally trained as an actor; mime was a skill that I had always had easy access to but didn't develop until after my drama school training. Developing my mime and movement skills helped me as an actor and, over time, I saw just how much stage and screen acting could be improved by applying my understanding of mime.

Firstly, mime does not have to be large, physical movements and expression. There is potential to 'do' mime like Chi Gung 'does' martial arts; there is an inner movement – a breath, a thought, an impulse, a flow of energy that screen in particular picks up well. Some actors have enough self-awareness in their early careers to be able to sense these movements; others grow into it. Learning mime encourages self-awareness to develop so that the smaller, inner movements can be sensed, honed and applied to perform with honesty and in the present moment.

Secondly, the principles of mime enable an actor to be more concise in their actions, their character physicality and their timing, without having to consider the emotion or backstory of a character.

Thirdly, it's very easy to create a bigger impact when a piece is directed using mime principles. They can make the stage/screen play 'tighter' and make life a little easier for actors who have little rehearsal time to develop their characters.

An exercise that I sometimes use when directing theatre helps actors find a way to genuinely respond to a situation or piece of dialogue, and it gives them a chance to create their own impulse so they can

OPPOSITE: Motion capture: movement for the Avengers Ultron, working with Andy Serkis.

speak their text honestly. A simple example: you are looking for your house keys – so check your pockets with big movements. Stop in a fixed point, and then speak the line: 'Did you take them?' Double-check your pockets and stop in a fixed point again to say the second line: 'This is the last straw!' You can move OR speak, but not do both at the same time in this beginning stage. (Verbal and physical comedy can easily be created using a similar method.)

Note: at the beginning of the exercise we make the physicality of the example exaggerated and then make it smaller and smaller until the actor feels the impulse of the action and can replicate it in following performances.

The actor will then run the scene as they were and will experience a new way of doing things having done this exercise. If we have the time, we can explore how this exercise can add new dimensions to the character and the text without the actor having to analyse either.

You can start to pay attention at how actors use movement on screen. A lot of movement (particularly in period dramas) happens before or after the text is spoken. It's easy to clean up your performance by practising this for yourself.

Humans are always moving and talking without being conscious of doing one or the other. When teaching an exercise that teaches the practice of paying attention to speech and movement, actors often struggle with it: separating speech and movement can feel very mechanical and fake. Yet when it's time to perform the scene, the narrative becomes very clean, precise and uncluttered. Once they have mastered this exercise I ask them to do the scene again and move and speak when they feel the impulse to do so. The exercise is a starting point that forces a limitation onto actors so they become aware of their movement and speech. The more they do the exercise, the more aware they become of isolating both and doing it in a natural way.

Ultimately the actor should follow their own impulses and playfulness, so they use their own sense of when to move or when not to move. Directing with mime principles helps actors fine-tune that intuition. And sometimes actors just need to be aware of their own habits of doing too much when they can do so much less.

A useful exercise to learn lines and develop character in your own time is to physicalize each word or sentence. Doing this with Shakespeare is great with his metaphor and can help in finding the tempo and rhythm of the text. As a director, it can also be interesting to see actors play with movements that could happen before and after a character's lines. This can offer new insights into the characters and the text and frees up actors so they are not stuck in the emotion or cognitive understanding of the scene. This is a simple thing you can implement in your own project or at home. Add a movement before and after each one of your lines – walk across stage, look in another direction, manipulate a prop, even blinking will help you discover more.

PLAY FIRST

Although Mime is a technique, I believe the most important thing is the actor's natural impulse and intuition. It is easy to clean up the movement when an actor is playing freely and honestly first. Coming from a movement background, I watch the body language and movement in the piece. Does the body want to move impulsively, but the actor isn't going with it? Is the actor moving too much to make it seem like they are doing something interesting on stage? By questioning these movements after an actor has played it in their own way helps them either to go with something that does work, or to cull what is unnecessary.

I recently directed an actress working on her monologues for screen and stage castings. She had already done a lot of work on the piece and asked

for feedback and direction to make them more successful in auditions. Whilst her performance was already good, with a few simple directions such as 'Slow your walk here,' 'Extend your arm movement there' and 'Let your movement carry your voice in this section,' the performance went from good to excellent, and she felt that it was much more powerful. As a consequence, with her newly structured monologues, she went off to secure a presence with a well-known theatre company. Applying mime principles can also be done after an actor's own work.

MOVEMENT AND TEXT

When watching a performance in rehearsal, I'm focused not on what the actor is saying or how they are saying it, but on what I see and experience while they are speaking. An actor must first have the skill to speak articulately, but after that, they can say their lines anyway they want – the lines will take care of themselves if the actor releases them to their fullest expression. When an actor is focused on the character's internal feelings or thoughts, or they are thinking about how best to speak the lines, the performance can become heavy and laboured, spontaneity is lost and the speech is not connected to the body, so it can't be fully released. Introducing some movement exercises to the process can help an actor shift their idea of how they should play the character (especially if they view the character as physically rigid for some reason) and help them find how the voice can be used on the movement, which can create more vocal range and power.

MIME AND FILM

Theatre is ideal for physical expression as it can be a feast of visual story telling that uses the body as the main vehicle of narration; indeed, we have a wealth of theatre companies creating work like this. In film and TV, the camera picks up the minutiae that theatre doesn't, so far less movement is required to create a visually stunning body of work. Film is the medium for the 'Chi Gung' style of mime (mentioned in the first paragraphs of 'Mime for Stage and Screen').

Film is also a visual banquet, and this is the very reason I am so drawn to filmmaking, editing and directing. Film is completely different to the theatre: while theatre is a live experience, film is an immortal record of something captured from the past. The beauty of film is that so many principles from mime can be applied directly to the screen: fixed points, body isolations, gestures, postures and stillness. A film editor can edit the best physical moments captured on screen to make the actors' performance appear even better than it really was. Film editing is all about the rhythm of cutting one scene to the next, enhancing the narrative and directing the audience experience to feel what you want them to feel at any given time. As a film director, knowing what works in editing and what will not, I'm always looking first to see what the movement is within the frame. I do a storyboard first of the action, considering how the movement of the camera or the actor will enhance and add to the next shot. Making films is all about the movement or stillness of what is within the frame. Are the actors moving and the camera still, or are the actors still and the camera moving, or maybe they are both in motion? They say in the film business 'everything that you see in films is 50 per cent sound'. That's right, sound is visual. As an example, a family is in the house and there is the sound of a baby crying in another room. We don't see the baby, but our mind registers its presence – we may see it in our mind's eye. So it is with mime. A mime artist creates the shape of a glass in their hand, pretends to drink from it and the audience 'sees' the mime drinking liquid from a glass.

When I direct actors for film I use a lot of fixed points and moments of stillness. One reason for this is because I know how I'm going to edit the film and how it will link up to the next scene. The second reason is that an actor needs to do far less than they think for the camera, and the fixed points and stillness are sometimes all the camera needs. The camera needs to see the inner moments and movements behind an actor's eyes, as

that is the very thing the audience will be looking at to understand the emotional journey of the character. It's nice if a film director can make the actor feel relaxed and physically free in front of the camera, but that doesn't always happen! You can apply some basic mime principles at the beginning of a screen acting career to help yourself. You need to be physically free and available on set so the camera doesn't pick up any discomfort (even if your character IS uncomfortable!) Your voice needs to reach only the microphone – not a theatre audience – but it still needs to be connected to your body so it doesn't come across as tense. Use some soft fixed points and subtle slow motion – a look or moment of stillness can be all that is needed to convey mountains of meaning and make an easy job for an editor.

MIME AND BEING YOURSELF

In all of my creative work as a performer, teacher and director, I have discovered it's all about giving yourself and your fellow artists the permission to be yourself. Great work comes from failures and freedom. Being relaxed and free enough to take risks, make mistakes and fail miserably is liberating. Each time I teach or direct, I take risks as I search for a concentrated version of what I already know, and sometimes I fail miserably. Being comfortable in myself doesn't mean I don't get nervous and tense, I still do, but it does make me more comfortable with what didn't work. This allows me to learn so much from my failures that I become a better person and artist for it. Great work and a great life come from knowing yourself. Finding yourself within yourself. To be yourself, it's crucial to feel comfortable about your body, your movement, your impulses, posture and voice. Mime and movement encourage people to inhabit their body, to discover their limitations and break through them. Discovering your body helps you discover your physicality, sensuality and spirituality.

My philosophy is quite simple: Let the moment move you, so you can be moved in every moment.

CONCLUSION

Mime can make you more aware of your own physicality, and very visually aware of your surroundings and the qualities of movement in everything around you – in film, people on the street, even in telephone conversations! I could be sitting in a park watching a squirrel scampering around and I notice its quality of movement, its particular rhythm, how it might be hunting for food and leading with its nose. How it comes to a sudden stop in a fixed point when it thinks there is danger nearby. How it isolates its head from its body when it looks around still holding the food crumbs in its paws.

Mime can make you more active than most in life, and lead you to explore things you wouldn't normally consider. You can use mime everywhere you go. For example, if you are in another country and can't speak the language, then the natural response is to start to mime gestures to people. The classic one is miming to a waiter, who is some distance away, to tell them that you would like to pay the bill.

When out socializing, I am aware of my posture and stand up straight, opening the chest area and pulling my shoulders back. You can also do this at castings, auditions, interviews and teaching. It sends the message that you are open and available to conversations and possibilities on any level. On the opposite scale, if I am on a train or in a public place and I don't what to be noticed or disturbed, I pull my shoulders and chest in, put my head down and draw my physical energy inwards.

To move or not to move, that is the question. Sometimes stillness is all that is required. Listening to someone speak you might be very still, facing them and looking into their eyes. If you are teaching and want the class to be quiet without saying anything, stand up straight and remain still, moving only your eyes around the room with a serious expression on your face. This will usually make a class fall silent very quickly. You could also use large gestures with resonating, slow movements and a fixed expression: this also draws people's attention to you very quickly.

Mime is also about knowing when to move and when not to. How to precisely isolate movements so you can communicate and be effortlessly expressive in performance and in daily life. Mime can be used anywhere, at any time, by anyone.

Life gives birth to mime every second of the day, such as when babies imitate the smiles, waves and kisses they see from the people around them. Mime exists because we have physical form, because we move, because we express ourselves, because we want to communicate with each other, and because we have the capacity to demonstrate with our bodies, as artists do with their brushes. Because, as with every natural thing in the universe, we are capable of demonstrating great beauty and truth. Mime is connected to a deep, invisible part of being conscious, which some people may call spirituality.

Mime is all about creating a wonderful world, and anything our imaginations can come up with, using only the body. The beauty of mime is that you don't need a set, props, words or text, and you can create it all by yourself. Mime isn't just about learning to be trapped in a glass box or walking in the wind, it's about learning how to be creative physically and becoming expressive so you can tell your own stories. Etienne Decroux would say that mime is 'making the invisible, visible'.

Mime Artists (l–r): Rayo Patel, Courtney Day, Ellie Cummings, David Norton. Photo by Richard Knight.

BIBLIOGRAPHY AND FURTHER READING

Blesh, Rudi, *Keaton* (Secker and Warburg, 1966)

Bouissac, Paul, *The Semiotics of Clown and Clowning* (Bloomsbury, 2015)

Broadbent, R.J., *A History of Pantomime* (The Echo Library, 2006)

Enters, Angna, *On Mime* (Wesleyan University Press, 1968)

Gaulier, Philippe, *My Thoughts on Theatre* (Éditions Filmiko)

Griffin, Jonathan (trans), *The Memoirs of Jean Louis Barrault* (London Thames and Hudson, 1974)

Kipnis, Claude, *The Mime Book* (Meriwether Publishing, 1974)

Lecoq, Jacques, *The Moving Body* (Methuen 2000, 2000)

Lecoq, Jacques, *Theatre of Movement and Gesture* (Routledge Taylor and Francis Group, 2006)

Lust, Annette, *From the Greek Mimes to Marcel Marceau and Beyond* (Scarecrow Press, 2000)

Mawer, Irene, *The Art of Mime* (Methuen and Co Ltd, 1936)

Movie Icons, *Chaplin* (Taschen)

Quigly, Isabel, *Charlie Chaplin early comedies* (Studio Vista | Dutton Pictureback, 1968)

Rea, Ken, *The Outstanding Actor* (Bloomsbury, 2015)

Rolf, Bari, *Mimes on Moving* (Panjandrum Books, First Printing)

Stolzenberg, Mark, *Exploring Mime* (Sterling Publishing Co.,Inc. New York, 1979)

Stott, McConnell, Andrew, *The Pantomime Life of Joseph Grimaldi* (Canongate, 2009)

Wright, John, *Playing the Mask* (Nick Hern Books, 2017)

INTERNET REFERENCES

www.mimethegap.com
www.mimeartists.com
www.mimeworkshop.com
mime.info
https://www.britannica.com/art/mime-and-pantomime
https://en.m.wikipedia.org/wiki/Mime_artist

INDEX

RELATED TITLES FROM CROWOOD

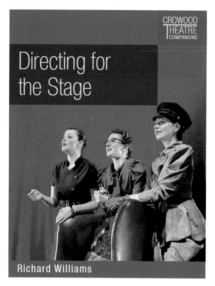

Directing for the Stage
ISBN 978 1 78500 379 20

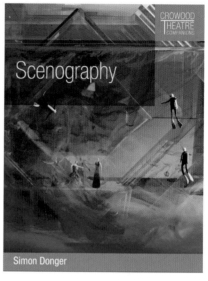

Scenography
ISBN 978 1 78500 453 7

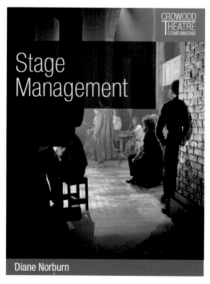

Stage Management
ISBN 978 1 78500 443 8

Theatrical Scenic Art
ISBN 978 1 78500 433 9

www.crowood.com